the
BAROQUE
prevalence
in
BRAZILIAN
art

LEOPOLDO CASTEDO

the BAROQUE prevalence in BRAZilian ART

CHARLES FRANK PUBLICATIONS, INC.
432 Park Avenue South, New York, N. Y. 10016

N
6650
.C3

Table of Contents

Architecture in Brazil, overcoming
the stage of orthodox functionalism,
is now in search of plastic expressions.
It is the extreme malleability of present
construction methods together with our
instinctive love for the curve—a real
affinity with the Baroque of our colonial
times—which suggests unfettered forms
of a new and amazing plastic vocabulary.

Foreword

Historian and art critic, Leopoldo Castedo, has let himself become enmeshed in a truly fascinating subject: Baroque predominance in Brazilian art. And he has dealt with it in an essay that, exceeding the objectives of history and art criticism, considers both the anthropological and philosophical implications of the subject.

He attempts to arrive at a definition of the Baroque through

Foreword

an analysis restricted to what may be called a *situated* Baroque —a Baroque associated, both in space and time, with specific collective (or national) predispositions of behavior and with conditions (also specifically collective) of coexistence: i.e., the essential traits of Brazil, both during a period of life still economically and politically pre-national (though national with respect to other socio-cultural and psycho-social aspects) —the period of Aleijadinho and of the colonial churches of Bahia— and during an already full-fledged national phase of Brazilian development —the period marked by the scenographic construction of Brasilia.

For Castedo, the chief attribute of the Brazilian nature is intuition. He does not, however, omit, as another distinguishing characteristic, sensuality —sensuality defined as "a capacity to feel and the gift of expressing such feelings"; a sensuality which, in Europe, animated virtually the entire "Baroque, Art of the Counter-Reformation," studied by Werner Weisbach, and inspired Spanish art itself despite that art's "abiding devotion to the ascetic."

In Brazil, in the religious art of Bahia, Leopoldo Castedo's analytical camera surprised —and masterfully photographed— details of angelic purity associated with "the tumescence of carnal forms," executed with that boldness and expressive self-determination that for him seem to imbue Brazilian art —or culture— with unequivocal traits. These are by no means traits common to the Hispano-tropical —or, from another standpoint, Hispano-American— complex to which Brazil, by virtue of several of its characteristics, belongs.

What is the reason for this Brazilian singularity which, for the astute analyst and critic, becomes a "dividing line" between the culture of Spanish America and Portuguese America? It is a subject worthy of study by a historian who is at the same time a well-qualified psychologist —a subject to be dealt with painstakingly and at leisure. I have tried to do this more than once in several of my essays. In one in which I tried to single out the first developments in medicine in Portuguese America from that of Spanish America, I brought out that, in Spanish America, medicine began to be studied —in the case of México— in universities, within the academic taxonomy in accord, by and large, with classic formulas through which native plants were studied. In Brazil, on the other hand, since the Portuguese had founded no university in their colony, European science or medical art was long represented by doctors trained in Europe who, however, for the most part, were surpassed in the treatment of tropical diseases by medicine men, experts in their familiarity with tropical diseases and plants and superior in this knowledge to academic doctors with exclusively European training. That was why —I suggested in that essay and reiterate it now— "that in Brazil, as in other tropical areas colonized by the Portuguese, tropicology had developed (with respect to its medical and pharmaceutical parts) in the same way that it developed with regard to architecture and cuisine: extra-academically." At least, more extra-academically

Foreword

than in Spanish America. If such a statement is accepted, would it not help explain what Leopoldo Castedo, based on his analysis of Baroque art in Brazil, considers a "boldness" and "expressive self-determination," a "freedom" characteristically Brazilian?

I also suggested in another of my essays that, for similar though not identical reasons, Brazilian sociology —in comparison to strictly classical sociology restricted to European formulas or Anglo-American techniques— may be considered a Baroque or Classico-Baroque sociology, as is the sociology of Euclydes da Cunha in *Os Sertoes*: a sort of equivalent, on the sociological plane, of the sculptures of Aleijadinho, the musical expressions of Villa-Lobos and the architectural forms of Lúcio Costa and Oscar Niemeyer. All these —sociology, sculpture, music and architecture— manifest themselves in those characteristically Brazilian feats of daring that are increasingly drawing the attention of Europeans and Anglo-Americans to the national culture of Brazil —works that, while they may be characterized as Classico-Baroque, may also be classified as Euro-tropical in general, Luso-tropical in particular.

It is impossible for us to disregard the fact that, in the expressionist rhetoric (rhetoric in the right sense) of Euclydes da Cunha, there are reminders of that of the Fernão Mendes Pintos —Portuguese with oriental or tropical, or oriental and tropical, experience; that, in the sculptures in the colonial churches of Brazil, there is a kinship with those in the Orient or in the Oriental Portuguese tropics; that, in Lúcio Costa —at least in Lúcio Costa— there is an assimilation of those Moorish and Arabic colors that the Portuguese so quickly adopted in his arts from his nearest non-European neighbor.

This Luso-tropical characteristic typical of Brazilian culture —including art— does not preclude the Brazilian Baroque, in its various expressions, from being one of Brazil's strongest links with the Spanish portion of the Hispano-tropical complex of *ethos* and culture. Indeed, Leopoldo Castedo notes that the "scenographic value" acquired by the Baroque in Europe, in Brazil "beggars the imagination," but he adds, "this phenomenon, where the extent and importance of ornamentation is concerned, is also common to Spanish America."

Mr. Castedo's observation that "Ibero-America was to act as a crucible in which a luxuriant nature, the Iberian background and the contribution of the Indian and Negro (early accentuated by hybridization and miscegenation) were to be fused" indicates that the Hispano-American perspective is not wanting in his analysis. From this standpoint, in his admirable essay (accompanied by the most expressive photographs ever to illustrate a publication on the prevalence of the Baroque in Brazilian art), the author emphasizes that, though throughout the Brazilian Baroque there are clear indications of a specific Brazilian *ethos* and culture, the universal seeking or yearning for infinitude is not missing in them.

Gilberto Freyre

1/defining the Baroque

Dynamism and delight in the curve, theatricality
and the breaking up of symmetry, unfettered
imagination, lyricism, sensuality . . .
all are attributes of the Baroque

The *capoeira* is an authentic Bahian dance stemming directly and uncontaminated from Africa. Like all traditional choreography, it tells a story[1] —the age-old struggle between the slave and the enslaver. But the dance, imbued with plastic feeling as but few are, has become so stylized as almost to have created a school. Today it is a pantomime of languid muscular fluidity in which the cat-like movements of the dancers at times freeze into a truly sculptural group: the writhings of the Laocoön are here impromptu, spontaneous flexings of the body.

The popular maestros, Pastinha and Bimba, deans of the capoeira, incorporate in their ever-changing art innumerable attributes of baroque expression —the dynamism, the delight in the curve, the open form, the theatricality, the tension, the breaking up of symmetry.

Yet the capoeria is just one example, as we shall show, of a baroque style prevalent in all the art forms of modern Brazil but perhaps best epitomized by that country's unique contribution to modern

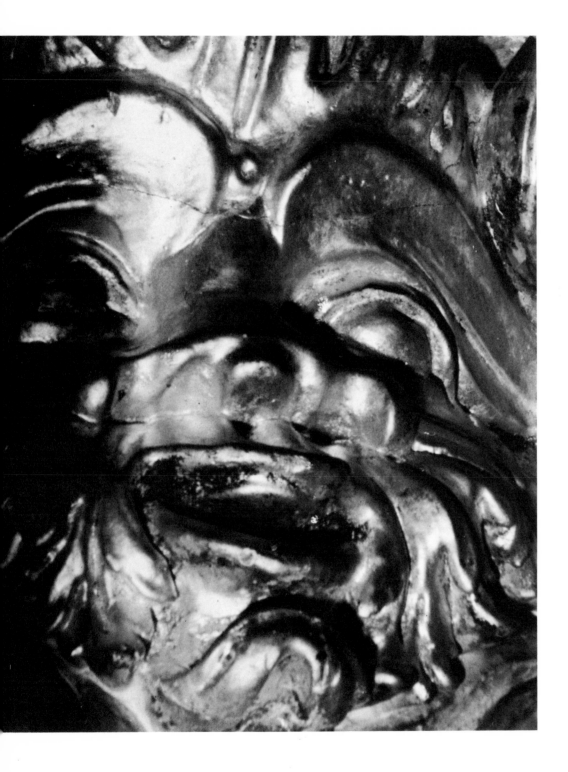

art —its architecture: more specifically, that exciting conjunction of audacity and unfettered imagination, of richness and variety, of lyricism and love of the curve —*Brasilia*.

However, before being able to single out any one style in any art form or work of art, we must first be able to recognize the characteristics or attributes that define the style —in the case of the Baroque, not an easy matter. Apropos of this, an observant Bahian journalist, Antonio de Assis Barros[2] called our attention to the use and misuse of the term. The most popularly accepted etymological interpretation is the one derived from the Portuguese and Spanish adjective disparagingly applied to a pearl cheaply held because of its excrescences and distorted form.[3] Others draw their interpretation of the term baroque from the scholastics who used the word *barroco* to describe a fallacious or absurd argument. Both connotations are extremely pejorative. The term baroque was (and for many still is) synonymous with the ugly, the twisted, the displeasing and, above all, the decadent.[4] It is not uncommon to find in French treatises on the history of art such titles as: "Seventeenth Century, France: The Resistance to the Baroque."[5]

In defense of the Baroque, we felt impelled to point out to Mr. Assis Barros at the time that if the term denotes passion, such a quality alone justifies the enthusiasm with which many of its lauders judge as baroque anything even remotely antithetical to classic beauty. Wherever there are complications, confusion or rhapsodizing, there can be detected —either covert or patent— the sensual, writhing spirit of the Baroque. All excess is baroque, and so, too, is all distortion of geometry. If, in the midst of so many exaggerations, we accept the idea that the Baroque is indeed complicated and confused, then picture the mountain of difficulties we must surmount in defining it —difficulties, incidentally, which can be gauged from the abundant bibliography on the subject.[6]

The paths proposed to define the Baroque are three: consideration of the Baroque as a historical period; evaluation of the Baroque as the final stage in the evolution of a stylistic period; identification of the supposed baroque spirit with certain specific national predispositions or traits, particularly among the Germans, Bohemians, Portuguese, Spanish and, above all, the Ibero-Americans.

The first —consideration of the Baroque as a historical period— is doubtless the smoothest, the least subjective, the one offering the simplest means of comparison. According to this line of reasoning, the Baroque is a historical style, a manner of seeing, doing and expressing which conditioned Western creativity from the mid-sixteenth to the mid-eighteenth century.[7]

The second path proposed, which has a host of advocates —tacit in Spengler, hinted at in Riegl, patent in Wörringer and popularized throughout the Hispanic world by Eugenio d'Ors— is that of considering the Baroque as the final stage of any style.[8] According to this hypothesis, where an artistic process was formerly divided into archaic, classic and decadent stages, these divisions are now labeled primitive, classic and baroque.

If the validity of both these paths is accepted, the term Baroque will have acquired an ambivalence similar to that of the term Romantic. Not only are both not contradictory, but they actually complement each other. In this sense, new values are acquired by the Spenglerian dualism of ethos vs. pathos, of Apollo vs. Dionysus, of reason vs. feeling (Gefühle). Gebhardt[9] sought to establish a rhythmic series of alternances in the essence of each style which might well correspond to this dualism: styles which are rational, symmetrical, plain, sober, preponderantly horizontal —i.e., the Romanesque, the Renaissance, the Neo-classic— giving place to styles that are extravagant, grandiloquent, confused, dramatic, vertical —the Gothic, the Baroque, the Romantic. For Gebhardt, thus, the historical sequence in art is a jagged line oscillating between the extremes of a restrained style and an unrestrained one.

We must still cover the third path in our attempt to define the Baroque —that is, the coinciding or identification of essential baroque attributes with certain specific national predispositions or traits. This is the path least studied, the riskiest and, to us, the most exciting.[10] In following this path, we must take into account those presumed values

or national characteristics which could be used to trace the course of the French, English, Germans, Bohemians, Austrians, Hungarians, Flemish, Iberians and Ibero-Americans through the pages of modern history.[11] From an over-all view of their works, we can agree that the basic premises of classicism (clarity, reason and symmetry) tend to reflect the spirit of the French, English and, perforce, the North Americans to the same degree that passion, fantasy, extravagance, complexity —in other words, the basic attributes of the Baroque— are the hallmark of the works of the Central Europeans, Iberians and Ibero-Americans. Poised on the fulcrum, like models of artistic equilibrium, are the Italians, leaning now to one side, now to the other, following the vagaries of a style launched by them as far as the Renaissance and the historic Baroque are concerned, but with an abiding penchant for classicism which has persisted in the depths of their consciousness since the days of Hellas.[12]

The Iberian, with his Romantico-Baroque predisposition, and the Anglo-Saxon, with his Apollonio-rationalistic predisposition, seemed to have sensed intuitively the sort of Nature fate had reserved for them in America as the setting for their colonization: for the Anglo-Saxon, spreading plains, accessible and similar in economic potential and climate to the subjugated earth of the Old World he was abandoning; for the Iberian, forbidding mountains, torrid heat, maddening distances and the savage jungle or desert.

Whether by chance or predestination, these differentiating conditions were to multiply their effects: the temperament transplanted to America was intensified by the respective environment. Ibero-America was to act as a crucible in which a luxuriant nature, the Iberian background and the contribution of the Indian and Negro (early accentuated by hybridization and miscegenation) were to be fused. In Brazil, particularly —and this is what matters here— the effects introduced by the climate[13] and by the precious contribution of the African[14] proliferated. Nonetheless, these were not the only departure points for the manifest differences between Portuguese and Spanish America. With

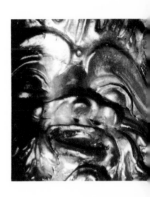

respect to Brazil's art history and particularly that of its architecture, the formal parting of the ways occurred as a result of markedly antagonistic constants, as we shall see below.

If the Baroque means depth (open as opposed to closed forms), if spatial feeling in the strict sense of structure defines baroque architecture, Hispano-American Baroque is not Baroque at all. Mario Buschiazzo, indubitably one of the most thorough and severe analysts of Ibero-American colonial art, after exhaustive research, found only three or four oval ground plans among the thousands of churches in Spanish America.[15]

Brazil, on the other hand, in the two forms of its colonial architecture —that of the littoral, linked to Europe, and the more independent one of Minas Gerais— maintains to varying degrees the formal tie with its Old (baroque) World, from the Portuguese São Pedro dos Clérigos in Recife to the incomparable achievements of Aleijadinho.

For the sake of our hypothesis, we must single out one more attribute of the Baroque —the most salient among its essential traits: that is, the tendency to intermingle the fine arts; the reciprocal subjection of architecture, sculpture, painting, music, poetry, drama and the dance to the advancement of a common ideal —the hallmark of the epoch and, consequently, of the style.[16] This yearning to achieve a community of form and expression is very old.[17] Where the plastic arts are concerned, however, the fusion (which often culminates in confusion) occurred for the first time in the Baroque period —and possibly nowhere more unmistakably than in the art of Brazil.

2/the Brazilian expression of the Baroque

*Universality, an intimacy with the divine,
sensuality and audacity—national characteristics
of the Brazilian people—are distinguishing
traits of the Baroque as well*

To identify the Baroque in Brazilian art, we must first risk a summary evaluation of those traits of the Brazilian people expressed in large measure in their art history. However, this is neither the time nor is there the space to try to compress here all that is so copious and valuable in the works of such outstanding authors and sociologists as Gilberto Freyre, Sérgio Buarque de Holanda, Euclides da Cunha, Érico Veríssimo, Jorge Amado and others.[18] Nonetheless, it would be wise to summarize some of their evaluations and interpretations of the Brazilian character.

There is no intention here of dogmatically stating a few facile generalizations —of which the most common is consideration of Brazil as a multifaceted continent. Unquestionably, the traits of the Northeasterner, the Mineiro, the Paulista, the Carioca, the Brazilian from the backlands and the one from the plains are sometimes completely different. But it is undeniable, too, that all Brazilians have certain traits in common which they have expressed artistically, since the earliest

Universality

Intimacy

Audacity

Sensuality

the Brazilian expression of the Baroque

flowering of the Luso-American Baroque, with a consistency seldom met with elsewhere.[19] These psychological attributes of the Brazilian people coincide —perhaps with greater force than in any other American group— with the basic themes of the historic Baroque.

Among the many traits to be deduced from the writings of the authors previously mentioned (melancholy, cupidity, sexuality, affection, liveliness, kindness, tolerance, quickness to act, universality, intimacy with the divine, sensuality and audacity), we propose to evaluate only the last four because we consider these as the most distinguishing of the traits and because their particular or identifying quality best coincides, in our opinion, with equivalent attributes of the Baroque.

However, before entering in earnest on a formal analysis of those which we consider most fundamental, we would like to add (from the abundant bibliography on the subject) certain other defining characteristics prevalent in the Ibero-American expression —but especially in the Brazilian expression— of the Baroque. Pre-eminent among these are the breaking up of outlines, the obsessive predominance of the curve and the evolution from a static and clean-lined equilibrium toward a dynamism which, in its self-delectation, borders on frenzy. All these become the defining characteristics signalling the transition from the Renaissance to the Baroque in all the arts but more manifestly in architecture, traditionally the head of the hierarchy.

It is well known that from the structural standpoint, baroque architecture is based on Greco-Roman lines as revitalized by the Renaissance.[20] This Classico-Baroque dualism, this superimposition of values with the alternating predominance of first one and then the other, acquired in Brazil, as early as the 17th century, an individual —and therefore unmistakable— form. In Hispano-Colonial architecture, from the discreet hints of the Plateresque,[21] the characteristic *altarpiece-façade*[22] of the churches is maintained. In Brazil, the façade is more severe. The dynamism is barely expressed in the volutes of the *imafronte* (pediment), the onion-shaped cupolas of the towers, the graceful framework of the lanterns. The sole exception to this is the façade of the Church of the Tertiary Order of São Francisco in Bahia. On the coast, the floor-

The altar-piece façade of the Church of the Tertiary Order of St. Francis in Bahia is in contrast to the severe façades of most Brazilian churches.

*The simple façade
of the Church
of São Francisco
(immediate left)
shows the discreet
use of baroque
elements over the
classical outline.
At the far left,
the Church of
Nossa Senhora da
Candelária in Rio
is one of the few
Brazilian churches
built with a dome.*

plans are quadrangular with the apse, also quadrangular, used as a sacristy and sometimes taking up the entire width of the temple. There are rarely domes. São Pedro dos Clérigos in Recife, Nossa Senhora da Gloria do Outeiro in Rio de Janeiro, Nossa Senhora do Rosário in Ouro Preto, São Pedro in Mariana, the destroyed São Pedro dos Clérigos in Rio de Janeiro and (with respect to the dome) the monumental Candelária[23] in Rio de Janeiro are some exceptions to the rule.

So much for the exterior of the churches in Brazil. When the worshipper enters the temple, the panorama undergoes a bedazzling change. The spatial character of the German Baroque is here transformed into a sensual, tangible, phantasmagorial lavishness. The stage-setting quality which in Central European churches is reduced into an enveloping illusion that leaves the spectator in the center, lost and bewildered, in Brazil is reduced as if by magic into the decoration and beggars the

*An example of the unrestrained and bedazzling use of ornamentation,
a baroque characteristic found in many of the colonial churches of Brazil.*

imagination. The theatricality typical of the Baroque here reaches the level of drama, confusion, bedazzlement.

The relative importance of ornamentation is common to all America of Iberian origin with the notable difference that in Hispano-American art, visualization is along a single plane. In Brazil, the enveloping movement as an expression of typical dynamism (characteristic of the Central European Baroque) culminates during the colonial period —as we shall see further on— in the work of Aleijadinho, but is present throughout its art history (with natural variations) as a happy constant —an unmistakable national trait— from the colonial *imaginería* to the sculptural integrations of Brasilia; from the pediments, broken into volutes, up to the undulant façades and the plastic exaltation of the dance of modern Brazil; from the draperies of Mestre Ataíde up to the twistings in Portinari's drawings; from the curly beards of Aleijadinho's *Profetas* up to the early Bahian Christs of Mario Cravo.

Another equally defining trait of the Baroque, which in Brazil attains exceptional proportions, consists in what a number of scholars have termed the artist's search for infinity. This value is concisely characterized for us by Hanspeter Landolt[24] when he speaks of the imaginative, theatrical character attained in the Bavarian churches, which "transport us to a world that is dazzling, ideal, incommensurate, lying outside our rational experience in an imaginary space, a space which does not obey the logic of the elements of gravity and thrust."

The search for infinity —carried to the sublime in Quevedo and El Greco, in Berruguete and the Passions of Johann Sebastian Bach— is made and achieved through the use of supra-realistic elements and with a squandering of fantasy which thus, of itself, acquires an intrinsic value. In Brazilian art, this baroque attribute is represented historically by a continuity in the concept of the grandiose —from the tremendous features with which Aleijadinho gives sculptural form to the biblical text to the spatial excess of the Plaza of the Three Powers in Brasilia, from the music of Lobo de Mesquita to the sublime *Bachianas* of Villa-Lobos, all examples of the most salient attribute in the search for infinity, namely, the esthetic value of timelessness. For the concept of

*The Church of Nossa
Senhora da Glória
do Outeiro in Rio
is one of the few
in Latin America
to be built
on the oval plan.*

infinitude defies representation. It is both timeless and beyond our concept of time. We can only draw near to it by giving full rein to our imagination, using fictitious elements that transport us beyond reality, beyond the realm of physics.[25]

The works of Villa-Lobos should be considered among the best to express this esthetic value of timelessness. The historical link between the great Latin American musician with the national baroque root is obvious. Villa-Lobos is an expressionist, not through imitation but out of affection. In his universal filiation he takes his place in the line initiated by Max Reger and made sublime by Hindemith. All are devotees of Bach. Villa-Lobos labeled his favorite works *Bachianas Brasileiras*,

a monument in their purity to the modern version of an intimate and profound Baroquism.[26]

Having sketched in those attributes of the historical Baroque which have been consistently manifested in the general characteristics of Brazilian art, we will now stop to evaluate the four basic, essentially baroque traits of the Brazilian people which we mentioned previously —namely, universality, intimacy with the divine, sensuality and audacity. First, however, we must point out that as the single supporting evidence of each of these national traits, we have merely chosen the most salient or representative example without meaning to imply in any way that it is the only existing proof.

3/ *Universality*

The prophets, Nahum and Joel, silhouetted against a darkening sky, bear witness to the universal values which Aleijadinho, Brazil's great sculptor, knew so well how to interpret in stone

How does the Brazilian national character express the universal, especially in its art?

The concept of universality in art is not only polyvalent but difficult to grasp —particularly if its analysis is approached from the standpoint of pure esthetics.[27] The distance between the capacity of the social group to express its collective self and the talent that makes it possible to confer universal value on this expression poses a dilemma characteristic of the history of culture. In this respect, among the Ibero-American countries, Mexico and Brazil unquestionably have held —and continue to hold— the commanding position.

Nearly all the attributes which we have previously stressed as being essentially and peculiarly Brazilian clearly distinguish and reveal the great creative capacity of this people. The Brazilian archetypes, drawing their substance from these peculiarly national characteristics, make it transcendental to all mankind. This capacity is more marked, without doubt, among the Iberians and Ibero-Americans than among

the other peoples who add distinction to the West of modern history.[28] Thus, the universal in the Mexican is epitomized by Chavez and Tamayo and in the Brazilian by Villa-Lobos and Niemeyer.

A happy coincidence of time, spirit and environment have added greater luster to the universal expression of what may be called a strictly Brazilian style. In the history of Brazilian art, the phenomenon is represented to perfection in the work of Aleijadinho. In the esthetic evaluation of this amazing figure, however, sentimental considerations concerning his life have hampered a dispassionate appraisal of his work. To understand better the historical factors that serve as a basis for our hypothesis, we must keep well in mind the circumstances under which this great artist lived and worked.[29]

Aleijadinho is a legendary figure and it is not an easy matter to disentangle the truth from the fable surrounding his person. Rodrigo José Ferreira Bretas, key documentary source on which all that has been written about Aleijadinho has been based, began his brief biographical work[30] a few years after the artist's death (in 1814) from an account given to him by the artist's daughter-in-law, Joanna Lopes, a midwife then living in Rio de Janeiro.

Aleijadinho was born in Villa Rica (Ouro Preto),[31] near the church where his remains are buried, on August 9, 1738 and was baptized Antonio Francisco Lisboa. He was the natural son of a Portuguese architect, Manuel Francisco da Costa Lisboa, who fathered him by a Negro African slave named Isabel and who gave him his name and declared him free on his baptism.

From his youth onward, Antonio Francisco was powerful of voice, impetuous of speech and wrathful of temperament. His complexion was the dark brown of a mulatto. His figure was chubby and ill-shapen and his head, covered with black kinky hair, was round and enormous with thick lips, large ears and short neck.[32]

Though Antonio Francisco knew how to read and write, Bretas does not record that he had any formal schooling other than that of

*Ouro Preto,
Minas Gerais,
birthplace
of Aleijadinho*

the excellent tutoring by his father and a profound familiarity with the Bible. The father, Manuel Francisco, enjoyed a well-merited reputation in Ouro Preto and vicinity as the best architect in the province and his son worked with him for many years. Tradition has it that the work of the son brought higher prices than the work of the father and teacher.

Up to the age of 39, Antonio Francisco enjoyed good health but, as might be expected from so bouyant and energetic a temperament, he soon squandered his vitality. Reportedly, he missed no opportunity to take part in all kinds of "vulgar dances" —with the logical consequences. From 1777 onward, his life was conditioned by diseases. According to the most widespread account, in that year, Antonio Francisco contracted the *zamparina,* an epidemic scourge that had spread throughout the region —a type of fever that produced convulsions and took its name from that of a famous Portuguese dancer in Rio who had so great a success that the fever was said to spread as quickly as the artist's fame. The medical name of this epidemic, which also ravaged vast areas on the Continent, is not known but its effects are: it was generally fatal; when it was not, the survivor bore for the rest of his days horrible deformities and was completely or partially paralyzed.

Other accounts maintain that Antonio Francisco was stricken with a combination of venereal disease and scurvy and not a few accounts claim that these maladies, dreadful in themselves, were further aggravated by leprosy. Whatever the origin and nature of the disease or combination of diseases, all the accounts[34] assembled by Bretas are in accord in noting the terrible stages of the pathological process in the artist. He lost all his toes and was thus compelled to walk on his knees. His fingers first contracted and clenched and then later atrophied. Most of them dropped off until only the thumbs and index fingers, which retained some slight movement, were left. The accounts reach their climax with the episode of his self-mutilation. Bretas relates that the terrible pain led Antonio Francisco to cut off his own fingers —using the same chisel with which he did his work. Later he had his work

tools strapped to the scarred stumps: the chisel to the left and the hammer to the right.

But his sufferings did not end there. He lost his teeth and his mouth became horribly twisted. It is easy to picture the fright which a meeting with such a monster could cause. According to one story, a slave whom he had just purchased to serve him as an assistant tried to commit suicide "to avoid having to serve so ugly a master."

Antonio Francisco also had another African slave, Mauricio, who worked as a carver and assisted him faithfully and zealously. Mauricio fitted the work tools to the stumps of his arms, the crippled man adjusting them only so that he could climb up and down the huge stairways that enabled him to reach the arches and altars he was carving. For this task, Antonio Francisco had himself fitted with two solid knee pads of leather. Two other slaves served him: Agostinho, also a carver, and Januario (the one who tried to kill himself) who was responsible for seating him on the burro that bore him to the churches far from his home or for carrying him on his back to those close by.

Antonio Francisco's prestige as an architect and sculptor, his terrible deformities and the creative drive whetted by his misfortunes, all conspired to create the to-be-expected nimbus of fame about his figure, not only in Minas Gerais but throughout Brazil. It was at this point that the people gave him the affectionate nickname of *Aleijadinho* —the "Little Cripple." What is most amazing is that Aleijadinho supposedly created his best works when he was without hands or feet.

The legend of the Little Cripple has remained fresh. Every year pilgrims from far away flock to the Church of Bom Jesus de Matozinhos in Congonhas do Campo (Minas Gerais) to testify to their religious faith in Aleijadinho's sculptures of the Prophets and the wood carvings of the Stations of the Cross.

We have chosen from this last work of Aleijadinho our example of universality because the supposed capacity to attain the universal is always closely allied with the quality and force of the genius. In

other words, our departure point is not from a presumed universal projection of Aleijadinho but rather from the ability of this isolated, unsociable mulatto to interpret universal values intuitively and give them form. The phenomenon is all the more remarkable if the circumstances are born in mind: adverse with respect to the possibilities of Aleijadinho knowing the outside world; favorable with respect to his freedom in expressing his intuitions.

The Church of Bom Jesus de Matozinhos rises on the crest of a hill, the "Morro do Maranhão." At the bottom, in the hollow, is the town. The slope leading to the sanctuary is steep. At the end of the houses, on the right, stands the circular building designed to house the pilgrims. Ahead, as he continues the climb, the pilgrim passes the six small chapels containing the Stations of the Cross. At the end are the

At the far left, Aleijadinho's Twelve Prophets look down upon the pilgrims coming to the Church of Bom Jesus at Congonhas do Campo. From the courtyard of the church (immediate left) the pilgrim can see the six chapels housing the Stations of the Cross and the village at the bottom of the hill.

staircase and the courtyard leading to the church. The spectator, standing on the central axis can see the twelve statues of the prophets in a single view. Drawing nearer, he can make out for the first time the choreographic intent of the artist, manifested in the three levels following the lines of the staircase. The courtyard is over 20 yards broad and rises nearly four yards in the front buttress (retaining wall). Masonry walls, plastered and whitewashed and capped by a cornice of *pedra sabão* (soapstone), form the balustrades. The simplicity of the curves gives an air of lightness to the structure as a whole. The Classico-Baroque dualism referred to in the opening chapters of this book is represented here by the contrast between the neoclassic symmetry of the balustrade and the baroque dynamism of the statues —life-size and standing on bases some eight inches high.

José de Sousa Reis, who has made the most masterly study[35] of

the Baroque prevalence in Brazilian art

Aleijadinho's courtyard of which we know, points out that the figures, cartouches and design are expressed as so many volumes of stone without being limited to a rigid naturalism. Nonetheless, though the soapstone (steatite) is easy to work, permitting a profusion of folds and the variety of a drawing, Aleijadinho maintained the means of expression appropriate to sculpture. For Sousa Reis, as for us, it is not a matter of a structure adorned with twelve statues. The resultant plastic creation is realized as a disciplined and architectonic conjunction of all the elements carved in the stone blocks. The interdependence of the statues and walls, of the forms and contours, uniting the elements of a single plastic creation, give Aleijadinho's courtyard its true quality of architectural monument. (Further on we shall see how an identical materialization of this body of concepts was realized a century and a half later in Brasilia.)

The ultimate aim of the work, concludes José de Sousa Reis, of complementing the external architecture of the church, contributed even more to the simplification of the form, shunning needless nuances and allowing the sculptures, thus stronger and more unified, to become part of the architectonic ensemble. So much for José de Sousa Reis's analysis.

Isaiah and Jeremiah flank the entrance to the stairway. On the next level, each enclosed in a small esplanade are Baruch and Ezekiel. On the third level, in the continuation of the stairway to the courtyard itself, stand the remaining eight statues: Daniel and Hosea look toward Isaiah and Jeremiah; Jonah and Joel[36] look toward the ends of the balustrade; completing the set, forming a sort of parapet, are the figures of Amos and Obadiah on one side, Nahum and Habakkuk on the other.

Each of the statues holds a cartouche bearing an inscription in Latin from a chapter in the Bible exemplifying the respective prophecy of the biblical figure. Here the previously alerted spectator receives his first surprise: each of the prophets reflects in his gesture the nature of his personality, from the seraphic kindness of Daniel to the wrathfulness of Isaiah; from the serpentine form of Ezekiel's arm, alluding

(continued on page 53)

*Daniel's calm face bespeaks his trust in God: "My God hath
sent his angel, and hath shut up the mouths of the lions, and they
have not hurt me: for as much as before him justice
hath been found in me ..."* (DANIEL 7, 22)

*The prophets, Hosea (left) and Daniel, look across at each other
from the highest point in the courtyard of the Church of Bom Jesus
where they form the central axis in Aleijadinho's "ballet in stone."*

*The serpentine curves of the whale, following the twisted lines
of the despairing Jonah, are in contrast to the simple,
peaceful figure of Amos, the prophet-shepherd, at right.*

Universality

Jeremiah,
severe of
countenance,
prophesies
the desolation
of Jerusalem:
"Therefore, behold
the days shall come
saith the Lord,
and it shall no more
be called Topheth,
nor the valley of the
son of Ennom,
but the valley
of slaughter . . .
And I will cause
to cease out of the
cities of Judea, and
out of the streets
of Jerusalem,
the voice of joy,
and the voice of
gladness, the voice
of the bridegroom
and the voice of the
bride: for the land
shall be desolate."
(JEREMIAH 8, 31-34)

Angrily, Isaiah announces
the destruction of the
world: "Behold, the day
of the Lord shall come,
a cruel day and full of
indignation, and of wrath,
and fury, to lay the land
desolate, and to destroy
the sinners thereof ...
For the stars of heaven,
and their brightness shall
not display their light:
the sun shall be darkened
in his rising and the moon
shall not shine with her light.
And I will visit the evils
of the world, and against
the wicked for their iniquity:
and I will make the pride
of infidels to cease ...
and the earth shall be
moved out of her place,
for the indignation of the
Lord of hosts, and for
the day of his fierce wrath."
(ISAIAH 13, 9-13)

With an implacable expression, Joel warns Judea: "...that
which the locust hath left, the bruchus hath eaten and that
which the bruchus hath left, the mildew hath destroyed." (JOEL 1, 4)

And the Lord told Ezekiel, "...say to the people
of the land...the cities that are now inhabited shall
be laid waste, and the land shall be desolate... (EZEKIEL 12, 20)

The left eye of
Habakkuk (photo
at the immediate
right) seems to
flash dire warnings
of the coming
destruction of
Jerusalem by
the Babylonians,
while his right
eye bespeaks
his trust in God:
"For though the fig
tree blossom not
nor fruit be on
the vines . . . Yet
will I rejoice in
the Lord and exult
in my saving God."
(HABAKKUK
3, 17-18)

At the far right,
the tranquil face of
Amos seems to say,
"I am not a prophet,
nor am I the son of
a prophet: but I
am a herdsman
plucking wild figs.
And the Lord took
me when I followed
the flock, and the
Lord said to me:
'Go, prophesy to
my people Israel.'"
(AMOS 7, 14-15)

Nahum predicts the fall of Ninive for "The Lord is a jealous God, and a revenger: the Lord is a revenger and hath wrath: the Lord taketh vengeance on his adversaries, and he is angry with his enemies ..."

(NAHUM 1, 2)

*The face of Hosea, like Daniel's, expresses his trust in God
though the Lord has said to him: "Go take thee a wife of fornications
and have of her children of fornications . . ."*
(HOSEA 1, 2)

the Baroque prevalence in Brazilian art

*Now the Lord
prepared a great
fish to swallow
up Jonah: and
Jonah was in the
belly of the fish
three days and
three nights . . .*
(JONAH 2, 4)

And Jonah prayed to the Lord his God out of the belly of the fish.
"I cried out of my affliction to the Lord and he heard me:
I cried out of the belly of Hell, and thou has heard my voice ..."
(JONAH 2, 2)

to the "horrible wheels," to the despairing curse and twisted neck of Jonah, the "defeated prophet," as Leon Felipe put it.[37]

The choreographic sense of Aleijadinho, which inspired one critic to call the group of statues a "ballet," is manifested in various ways and in different categories. In the figures of the prophets, a movement is suggested whereby the axis of the center of gravity is displaced. If the weight of the stone were neutralized, some statues would fall. In several of them, the movement of the feet corresponds to what in ballet is called the "third position." Moreover, the planted heels are at the precise moment of taking a step, in a startling anticipation of Rodin's Burghers of Calais. Another choreographic value is established by considering the statues, singly or as a group, beginning with the partial groupings by pairs, by threes or by fours and ending with the presentation of the entire group.

In the photograph at the far left (top), the prophets Amos, Baruch, Jonah, Ezekiel, Daniel and Hosea form a "ballet in stone," while in the photograph at the bottom left, the rear view of the statues clearly shows the dynamic displacement of the central axis. In the photograph at left, Joel's feet are shown in the ballet "third position."

4/ *Intimacy*

*The intimate, almost familial feeling for the divine
which is a common heritage of the Ibero-Americans
finds, perhaps, its best Brazilian expression
in the Stations of the Cross at Congonhas do Campo*

In his analysis on the permeability of·individual relationships, Leopoldo Zea[38] maintains that an Ibero-American aspect of this attribute is demonstrated by the typically Brazilian trait of tolerance. We believe that this attribute is raised to the level of the sublime in what we may call intimacy with the divine. Freyre notes: "The cultivation of this sentiment [tolerance] in a country predominantly Catholic is done gently, in the family circle, with a practically familiar relationship between the saints and men."[39] Such camaraderie with the divine is a common heritage of the Ibero-American peoples. The examples are legion, from Mexico to Paraguay; from the bas-reliefs of the Campaña in Puebla, where the birth of the Virgin is depicted in an everyday scene, with all the symbols of a domestic childbirth, to the siren playing the *charango*[40] on the façade of the Cathedral of Puno; from the saints in Indian garb in Peru to Saint Ferdinand wearing a derby and holding the globe in his hand in Venezuela.

The Iberian roots are noticeable in the sacred *imaginería* of

the Baroque prevalence in Brazilian art

Salzillo[41] and Martínez Montañés while the New World variants are to be found in the Indian background of Hispano-America and the Negro warmth of Brazil. Indeed, the extremes of this symbiosis extend, in Peru, to the Tiahuanacan figures of the Colegio Carolino (ex-Jesuit) of Cuzco and, in Bahia, to the rite of washing the front steps of the Church of Nosso Senhor do Bomfim which stems from both Catholic and African roots. This Luso-African syncretism in Brazil has multiplied the effects of the common roots in both the colonial and contemporary expression of this familiarity with the saints. Who judges as irreverent the Ibero-American's intimate attitude towards the divine betrays his ignorance of an admirable constant factor in the history of Ibero-America. The Catholic Church became an inextricable part of the soul of the people during the Ibero-American colonial period. The common man felt himself completely one with the religious sentiment and rite of the Church to such a point that in Ibero-America there occurred a complete fusion between the symbology of the Gospel and the people's capacity to express artistically what the Gospel represents to them and how it has permeated to the marrow of their bones.

In Brazil, the manifestation of this intimate yet devout sentiment is also embodied in the rustic carvings of Aleijadinho, which some critics consider complementary to the sculptural group in the courtyard of the Church at Congonhas do Campo. The Stations of the Cross are housed in six small chapels flanking the approach to the Church. The 67 statues of painted wood are grouped in seven scenes of the Passion of Jesus Christ: the Last Supper, with 15 figures; the Agony in the Garden, with 5; the Prison, with 8; the Scourging and the Crowning, assembled in a single chapel, with 14; the Road to Calvary, with 15, and the Crucifixion, with 10.

From the documentation assembled by the Serviço do Patrimônio Histórico e Artístico Nacional,[42] and especially by Germain Bazin in his last work on Aleijadinho,[43] we can gather that this artist worked on the seven groups as a contractor and director of the work. Numerous opinions have been raised which detract from the merit of the groups and deny a paternity which the documents clearly show. José Mariano Filho,[44] for example, in 1940, expressed an opinion that has been repeated later by many authors without being further verified. According to Mariano Filho, the workmanship is clumsy, "a number of characters are in an awkward attitude. . . . Of the wooden figures in the Stations of the Cross at Congonhas, I feel absolutely certain that Aleijadinho worked on only three. . . ."

Let it be said in exoneration of the many critics that the wooden statues they criticised bore very little relation at that time to the work entrusted to Antonio Francisco. Up to 1957, in fact, the beauty of the original workmanship of the 67 carvings remained hidden. In that year of grace, the Serviço do Patrimônio Histórico e Artístico Nacional transferred to Congonhas do Campo the amazing crew of restorers who, under the direction of Edison Motta, had restored to its original beautiful state the small jewel of Nossa Senhora do O in Sabará (Minas Gerais).

Lourival Gomes Machado and the photographer Eduardo Ayrosa have left us an admirable account of what was in its day the veritable "Reconquest of Congonhas."[45] Thick layers of paint, in repeated profanations, had converted this prodigy of popular religious imagery into the confused and bedaubed series of deformed and inexpressive beings mentioned by José Mariano Filho. The patient and scientific work of Motta and his group has returned to us the most priceless Brazilian expression of intimacy with the divine.

Experts argue over the paternity of the sculptures of the Stations of the Cross at Congonhas. There are three possible premises: 1.) that Aleijadinho acted as the contractor and only carved some —a very few— of the sculptures; 2.) that in the capacity of contractor, he personally created the best figures (the seven Christs, the twelve apostles of the Last Supper, the Magdalene, the three sleeping apostles, Saint Peter in Prison, among others); 3.) that he lovingly carved the best and then rapidly those that serve as supporting figures or simply to enhance the caricatural feeling (the big-nosed Roman soldiers, etc.).

*And while they were eating He said, 'Amen I say to you, one of you
will betray me.' While two of the apostles (left photo) gesticulate*

Regardless of which premise is correct, if Antonio Francisco
Lisboa was assigned the commission of carving the 67 figures and duly
collected for the work —and the documentation assembled by SPHAN
and by Bazin bears this out— then to him is due the acclaim or vituper-
ation. In the final analysis, if Aleijadinho was not the sole author of
these sculptures, they serve as still better proof of the typical Brazilian
feeling of intimacy with the divine for in this case even more merit, as
a collective achievement, must be credited to the combination of native

in surprise, John (right photo), the youngest of them and Christ's favorite, leans his head in sorrow against the Master's shoulder.

artists who knew how to interpret so masterfully the "familiar encounter with the divine" in Congonhas do Campo.

It would be presumptuous of us to attempt to describe in words the feeling of intimacy with the divine so expressively translated into concrete form in the 67 sculptures of the Stations of the Cross. We believe that the accompanying photographic study of these sculptures eliminates the necessity for literary comment which needs only be based on the biblical texts Aleijadinho interpreted so majestically.

the Baroque prevalence in Brazilian art

In the scene of the Last Supper, note the dynamic movement of the hands of the apostles forming a true Grecian fret.

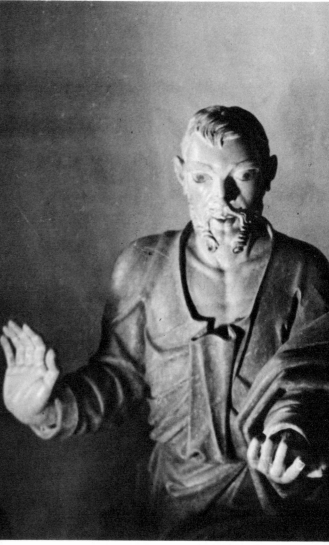

And being very much saddened they began to say, "Is it I, Lord? ..." (MATT. 26, 22)

But he answered and said, "He who dips his hand into the dish with me, he will betray me ..." (MATT. 26, 23)

"The Son of Man
indeed goes his way,
as it is written
of Him: but woe
to that man
by whom the Son
of Man is betrayed:
It were better
for that man if he
had not been born."
And Judas who
betrayed him
answered and said,
"Is it I, Rabbi?"
He said to him,
"Thou has said it."
(MATT. 26, 24-25)

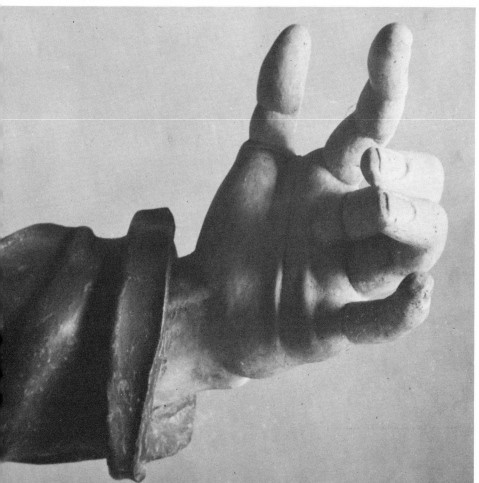

And he came out and went, according to his custom, to the Mount of Olives ... and kneeling down he began to pray, saying, "Father, if thou art willing, remove this cup from me; yet not my will but thine be done." And there appeared an angel from heaven to strengthen him. And falling into an agony, he prayed the more earnestly. And his sweat became as drops of blood running down upon the ground." (LUKE 22, 39-44)

Christ's hand is eloquent in prayer.

And he took with him Peter and James and John, and he began to fe
dread and to be exceedingly troubled. And he said to them, "My so
is sad, even unto death. Wait here and watch." (MARK 14, 33-3
Then he came and found them sleeping. And he said to Pete
"Simon, dost thou sleep? Couldst thou not watch one hour? Wat
and pray that you may not enter into temptation. The spi
indeed is willing, but the flesh is weak." (MARK 14, 37-3

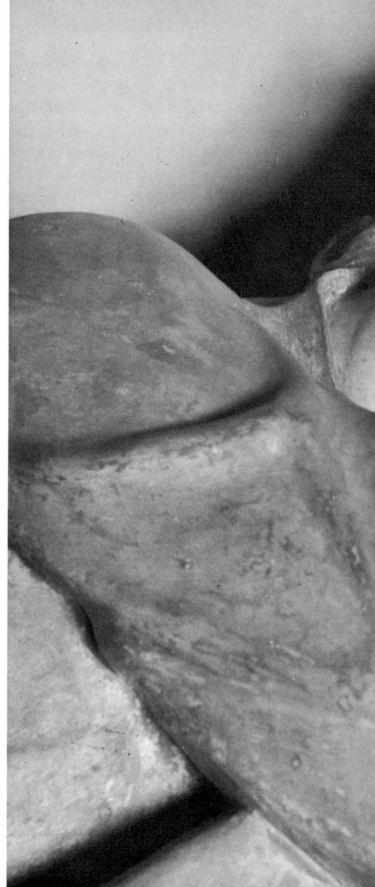

And he came the third time,
and said to them, "Sleep on now,
and take your rest! It is enough:
the hour has come. Behold, the Son
of Man is betrayed into the hands
of sinners. Rise, let us go. Behold,
he who will betray me is at hand."
(MARK 14, 41:42)

And while he was yet
speaking, Judas Iscariot,
one of the twelve, came
and with him a great
crowd with swords and
clubs, from the chief
priests and Scribes
and the elders.
(MARK 14, 43)

the Baroque prevalence in Brazilian art

*...and he drew near to Jesus to kiss him. But Jesus said to him,
"Judas, dost thou betray the Son of Man with a kiss?"*
(LUKE 22, 47-48)

*Simon Peter, therefore, having a sword, drew it and struck
the servant of the high priest and cut off his right ear.
Now the servant's name was Malchus. . . .*

*. . . Jesus therefore said to Peter, "Put up thy sword
into the scabbard. Shall I not drink the cup
the Father has given me?"* (JOHN 18, 10-11)

the Baroque prevalence in Brazilian art

*So Pilate, wishing to satisfy
the crowd, released to them
Barabbas; But Jesus he scourged
and delivered to be crucified.
Now the soldiers led him
away into the courtyard of the
praetorium, and they called
together the whole cohort . . .*
(MARK 15, 15-16)

*Then they spat in his face
and buffeted him; while others
struck his face with the palms
of their hands, saying,
"Prophesy to us, O Christ:
who is it that struck thee?"*
(MATT. 26, 67-68)

*And they stripped him and put on him a scarlet cloak and plaiting
a crown of thorns, they put it upon his head and a reed into
his right hand; and bending their knee before him, they mocked him
saying, "Hail, King of the Jews."* (MATT. 27, 28-30)

And when they had mocked
him, they took the purple
off him and put his own
garments on him, and led
him out to crucify him.
(MARK 15, 20)

And bearing the cross
for himself, he went
forth to the place
called the Skull, in
Hebrew, Golgotha...
(JOHN 19, 17)

The distress and astonishment mirrored in the face of Christ emphasize here the expression of innocence characteristic of all the seven statues of Christ found in the Stations of the Cross at Congonhas do Campo. The eyes, with their look of hurt interrogation, are the only ones of the seven statues to have dark pupils.

the Baroque prevalence in Brazilian art

Now there was following him a great crowd of women, who were bewailing and lamenting him. But Jesus turning to them said, "Daughters of Jerusalem, do not weep for me, but weep for yourselves and for your children. For behold, the days are coming in which men will say, "Blessed are the barren, and the wombs that never bore, and breasts that never nursed." (LUKE 24, 27-29)

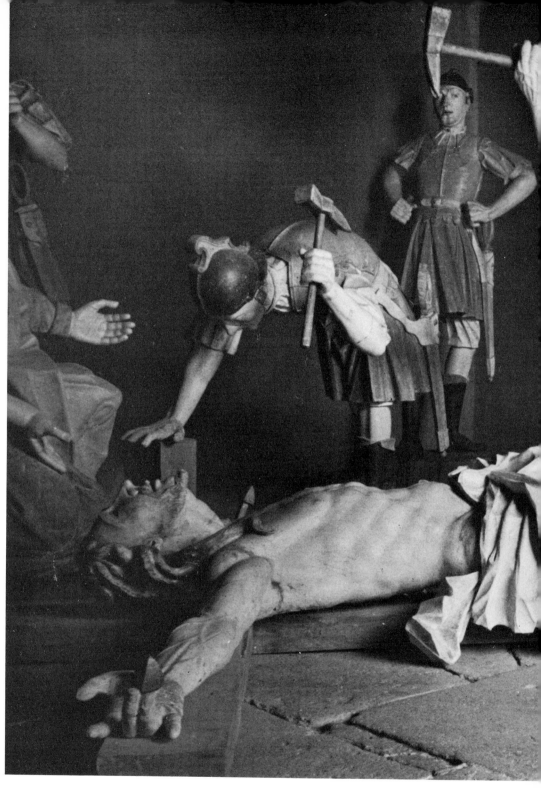

Now there were two other malefactors
led to execution with him. And when
they came to the place called the

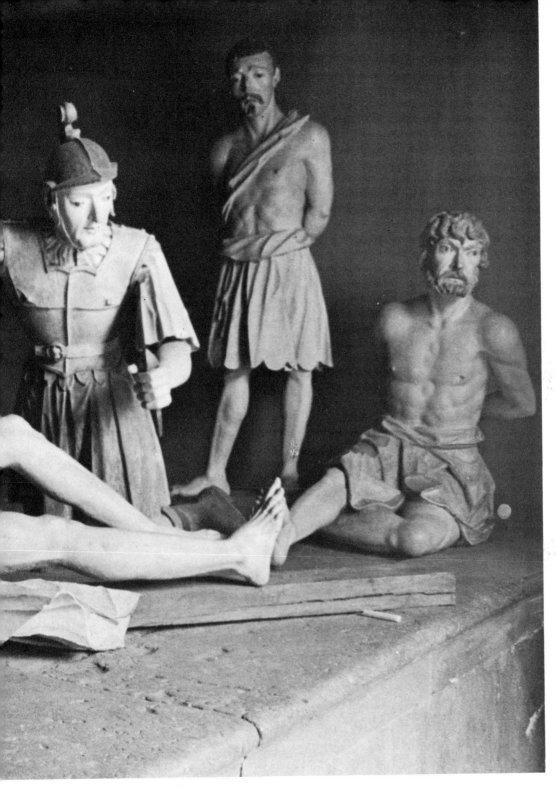

Skull, they crucified him there,
and the robbers, one on his right
hand and the other on his left. (LUKE 24, 32-33)

And after they had crucified him, they divided his garments, casting lots, to fulfill what was spoken through the prophet, "They divided my garments among them and upon my vestures they cast lots." (MATT. 27, 35)

Now one of those robbers who were hanged was abusing him, saying "If thou art the Christ, save thyself and us." But the other rebuked him and said, "Dost not even thou fear God, seeing that thou art under the same sentence? And indeed we justly, for we are receiving what our deeds deserved; but this man has done nothing wrong." And he said to Jesus, "Lord, remember me when thou comest into thy kingdom." And Jesus said to him, "Amen I say to thee, this day thou shalt be with me in paradise." (LUKE 24, 39-43)

*Now there was
standing by the
cross of Jesus
his mother and
his mother's
sister, Mary of
Cleophas, and
Mary Magdalene . . .*
(JOHN 19, 25)

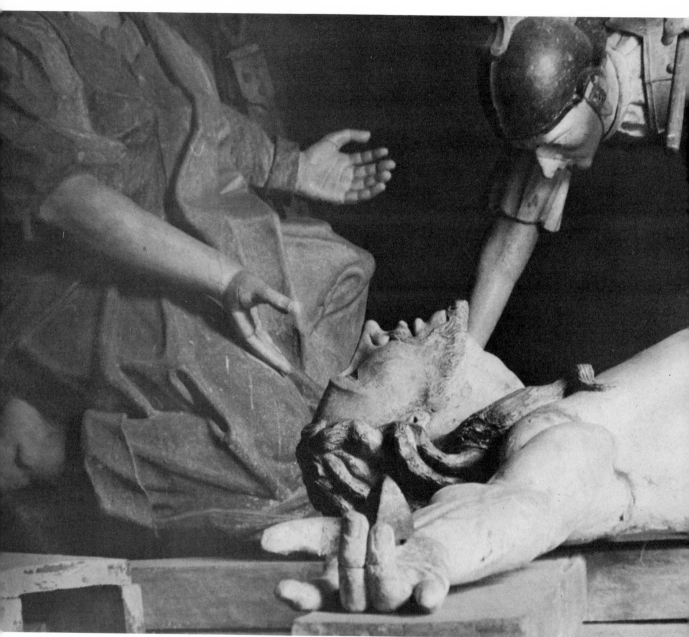

Now from the sixth hour there was darkness over the whole land until the ninth hour. But about the ninth hour Jesus cried out with a loud voice, saying, "Eli, Eli, lema sabacthani," that is, "My God, my God, why hast thou forsaken me?" (MATT. 28, 45-46)

Intimacy

And the sun was darkened and the curtain of the temple was torn in the middle. And again Jesus cried out with a loud voice and said, "Father, into thy hands I commend my spirit." And having said thus he expired.

(LUKE 24, 45-46)

5 / Sensuality

*There is nothing in the mind
which was not first in the senses*

Still another powerful and identifying characteristic of the Brazilian is sensuality. We refer, of course, essentially to the philosophic value of the term: *Nihil est in intellecto quod prior non fuerit in sensu*.[46] In esthetics and the history of art, this value signifies a delight in the awareness of the senses and skill in expressing that feeling.

This is not the place, nor is it our intent, to analyze the hedonistic forms in which the Ibero-American being is expressed. Our sole concern is consideration of Brazilian sensuality in its artistic expression, in its coincidence with certain traits of the Baroque and in a comparison of it with the manner in which sensuality is expressed in other times and other places.[47]

Werner Weisbach's work, "The Baroque, Art of the Counter-Reformation"[48] has become universal thanks largely to his appraisal of sensuality as a peculiar trait of style. The first part of this book is devoted to illustrating the artistic forms of this "longing and desire for sensual emotions." Even austere Spain —despite its abiding devotion to the ascetic[49]— expresses it: the cadaverous in El Greco, the marvelous creative coarseness of Quevedo, the allusions of Góngora, the

the Baroque prevalence in Brazilian art

materialization of mystic love and human grace which Murillo, according to Weisbach, attributes to the saints.

In Hispano-America, sensuality is manifested in art only as an inordinately proliferant and, therefore, baroque ornamentation, particularly in the Mexican popular churches with a strong Indian background (e.g., Santa María Tonantzintla or San Francisco Acatepec). An explanation for this may be found in Paul Westheim's interpretations of the pantheism in the ancient cultures of Anáhuac.[50] Only rarely —and then, hidden in places the researcher must painstakenly track down— will you find in some churches examples of the erotic: the siren concealed in the rear niche of the altar in the Golden Chapel of Puebla, for example.[51]

In Central America and the Spanish portions of South America there are no examples —even allusive ones— of eroticism nor any form of sensuality. The figural representation of the native fauna and flora in Arequipa, in the plateau of Collao and in Potosí is stylized, geometric and cold.[52]

In Brazil, in the northeast particularly, sensuality is more in tune with the depictions of Mary Magdalene, according to Vossler, or with the conflicts Weisbach attributes to St. Francis de Sales.[53] It should be kept in mind, however, that the force of the environment —the influences of its widely differing regions and climate— have differentiated the phenomenon within Brazil itself. The peculiar manifestations of Brazilian sensuality in its many forms (the cuisine, the clothing —or lack of it— the dramatic representation, the ornamentation) occur in a widely different fashion on the plateau of Minas Gerais from that of the hot coast. In the art of Minas Gerais, sensuality scarcely appears notwithstanding the propitious historical circumstances stemming from the confusion created by the "gold fever."[54]

As far as the contribution of the blood is concerned, the creative participation of the Negro was considerable in Minas Gerais (Aleijadinho and Ataíde. among many other masters, were mulattoes). The material most widely used, *pedra-sabão* (soapstone), which Lourival Gomes Machado accurately describes as oily, through the ease with which it

is worked and its tactile smoothness, delights the senses. Nonetheless, the art of Minas Gerais is not sensual.[55]

These arguments certainly do not run counter to Freyre's thesis as to the common traits of a ruling Luso-tropical civilization such as Brazil. On the contrary, they clearly support the differentiation that the Brazilian sociologist himself establishes (and of which he furnishes so many examples in the last-cited work[56]) in the interplay between the dionysiac and the ascetic. But, even more germane to our thesis is Freyre's study of the so-called "chaste nude."[57] During his last voyage to Africa he observed men, women and children in a state of semi-nudity or virtual nudity "not in the least obscene. . . . Perhaps this is why these people felt the need of aphrodisiac dances." On being christianized, they carve their saints, too, semi-nude and the Virgins as mothers covered only from the waist down. They also, therefore, create (or recreate) a Jesus as God become man in general —not a Jew or a Nordic in particular.

Ernani Silva Bruno recalls the surprise of the traveler Froger in Bahia when he happened upon a Corpus Christi procession with "musicians, dancers and maskers in lewd gambols."[58]

The most forceful example of sensuality in Brazilian art, however, is to be found in the leafy tracery of the altarpieces, pulpits, balustrades and carvings in general of the Brazilian coastal churches. Fairly often, the need for sensual release is not confined to the abundance and richness of display. At times it skirts the borderline between the sensual and the sexual in the carvings inside the church —with no blushes on the part of either the artist or the parishioners. Examples of this sort can be found in the Church of the Tertiary Order of Carmelites in Cachoeira (probably made by the same hand as the carvings in the Church of São Francisco in Bahia); in a side altar of the former Church of the Jesuits, now the Cathedral, in Bahia; in the stone sirens adorning the principal portico in São Pedro dos Clérigos in Recife and, most of all, in the pulpits and transept of São Francisco in Bahia.

Germain Bazin has made a painstaking, comparative study of the

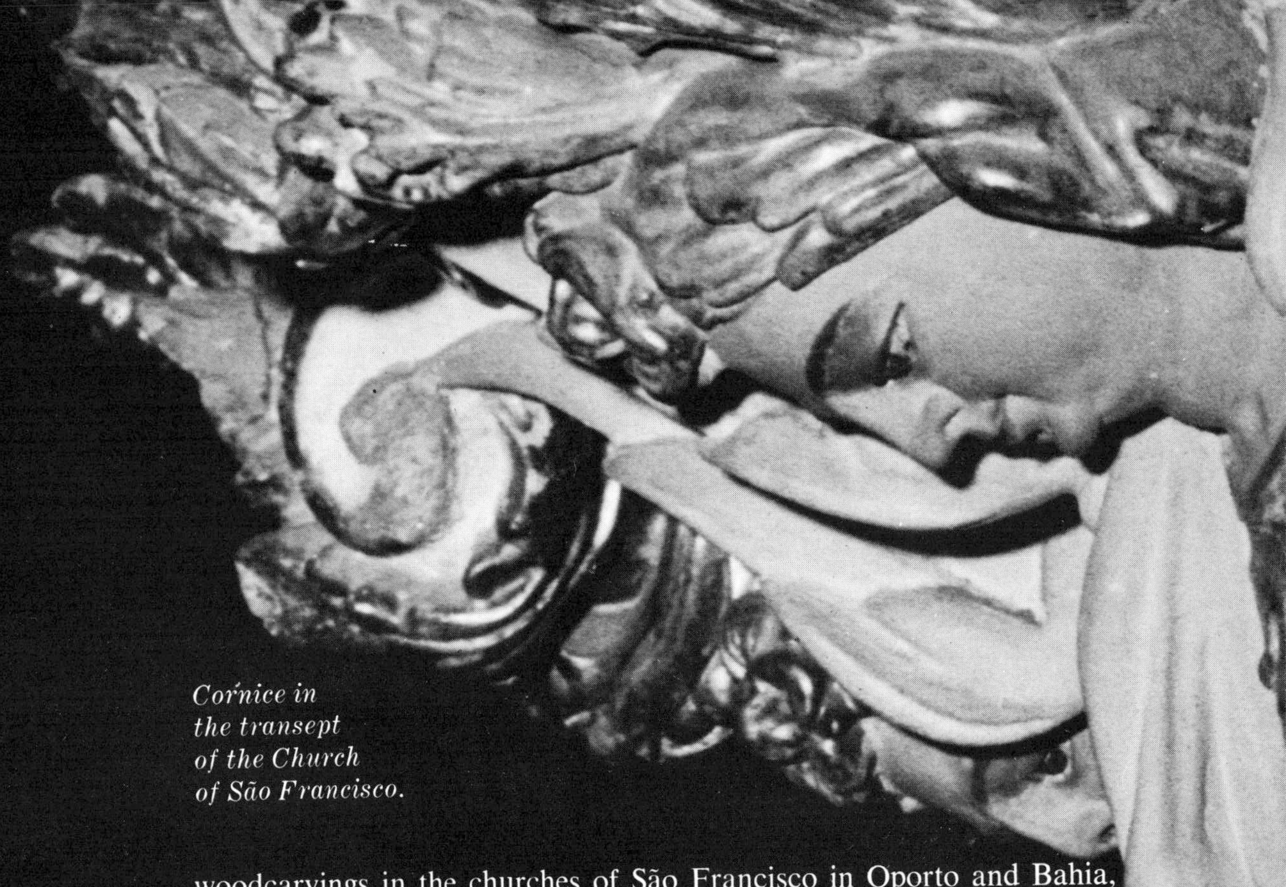

*Cornice in
the transept
of the Church
of São Francisco.*

woodcarvings in the churches of São Francisco in Oporto and Bahia,
which he considers "the greatest undertakings of their kind in all Portuguese art."[59] The two churches exhibit a similar colossal use of many
colors, but the sensual traits are more clearly marked in Bahia. Robert
G. Smith points out that the sacristies mark "an achievement peculiar
to Colonial Brazil, carried to its apex in Bahia."[60] This opinion on the
specific value of Bahian art is matched by a similar dithyramb to the
sensuality of the ornamentation, especially in the small pulpits of the
nave preceding the transept in the Church of São Francisco. Literary
description could never convey the true force of the spectacle. Carved
angels, exhibiting all the feminine attributes of pregnant women and
ostentatiously displaying the least ascetic forms of such attributes,
decorate the aforementioned pulpits and walls of the principal arch.[61]
Here the borderline between sensuality in the abstract and eroticism
vanishes. The spectator from another latitude is dumbfounded to see
that between each pair of *heterae* is a faun of openly lecherous expression. Though it carries the example to extremes, it represents one more
substantiation of the value attached by the Brazilian, as a man of the
tropics, to a shared innate sensuality.[62]

The most forceful examples of sensuality in Brazilian art are to be found in the pulpits and transept of the Church of São Francisco in Bahia: note the earthy, red-nosed cherub (above); the angel supporting a canopy while unsteadily balanced over a vault (left).

*Sensual female forms and satyrs lurking amidst the foliage
adorn the right pulpit of the Church of São Francisco in Bahia.*

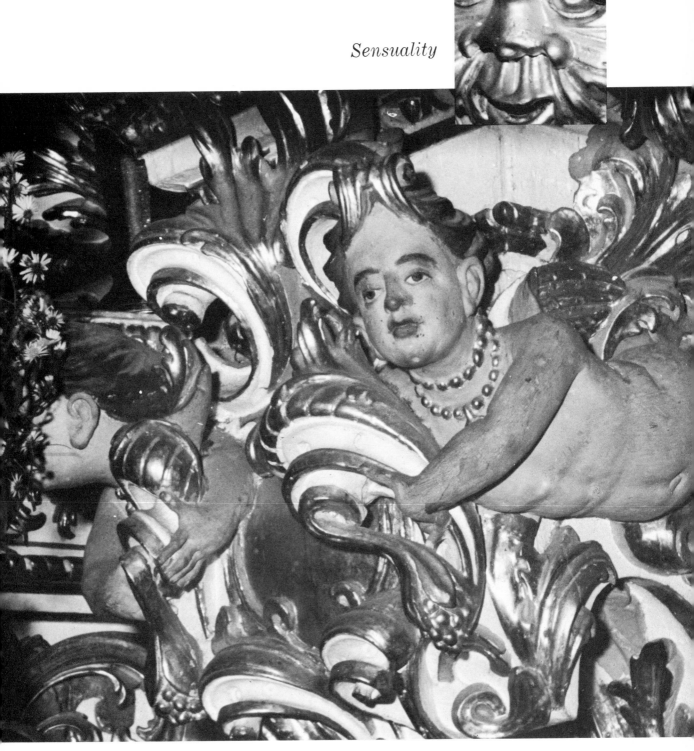

*Two earthy cherubs hold the volutes of a column
in the transept of the Church of São Francisco in Bahia.*

a pulpit in
the transept of
the Church of São
Francisco in Bahia.

A demon glowers amidst the carvings in the rosewood furniture
of the sacristy at the Church of São Francisco in Bahia (left)
while (below) a voluptuous angel substitutes for a baluster
in the balustrade of the central aisle of the same church.

6 / *Audacity*

Daring to break with conventional molds;
the feeling of virtually unlimited plastic freedom
in revolt against functionalism: these are
characteristics of the Baroque—and of Brasilia

The preceding analysis has illustrated the persistence in Brazilian art of an obsessive idea of doing violence to reality —even to the point of the most unheard of and spectacular formulas. This idea manifests itself through a daring, self-determination and creative freedom made even more conspicuous by the Brazilian trait of audacity. In the field of artistic creation, audacity implies the ability to break with conventional molds and relentlessly attack the conventional. Historically, this characteristic reached sublime heights in the work of Aleijadinho; in modern times, its greatest expression is to be found in Brasilia.

This path leads us to enlarge upon a thesis put forth by the Brazilian architects, Lúcio Costa and Oscar Niemeyer, i.e., the need in architecture for an equilibrium between form and function, of a hierarchic equalization of both attributes. These attributes, especially characteristic of architecture, are expressions of the great collective attitudes: of the highpoints in man's encounter with his epoch and, above all with his own collective self —that is, with his national or, in the case of the Ibero-American, continental soul.

The curves of the flying buttress of the Palace of the Planalto
in Brasilia contrast with the straight soaring lines of the
Congress Administrative building towers.

the Baroque prevalence in Brazilian art

In the opinion of Lúcio Costa[63] the importance of modern architecture lies in its capacity to arrive at an equilibrium between the plastic quality and the lyric and emotional content of the architectonic work. In this statement, which today bespeaks a visible reality, is contained several of the basic points we had attempted to make previously. The lyric and, above all, emotional qualities are primary attributes defining the very essence of the Baroque. In this, the continuing link with Brazil's colonial traditions is made even more evident by the skipping over of French neo-classicism in the art of Brazil's empire period —a Gallicization which never succeeded in destroying the 18th century tradition in civil architecture.

The virtual paralysis of architecture during the 19th century ties in perfectly with our theory of a baroque prevalence in Brazilian art. In 1809, the court of Dom João VI, prince regent and subsequently emperor of Portugal, was established in Rio de Janeiro. Seven years later the artistic leadership of Brazil was placed in the hands of the painter Lebreton who headed a group of French architects, painters and sculptors charged with the task of "civilizing" the country.[64] The New Imperial Academy appointed as director the French architect, Auguste-Henri-Victor Grandjean de Montigny who designed the Imperial Academy of Fine Arts, the Market and the Customhouse in keeping with the most polished neo-classicism. This French superimposition on the Brazilian spirit soon became a dividing factor.[65] Architecture took two antagonistic paths: one following the "native" and popular Portuguese tradition; the other adopting the new imported fashion.

Towards the end of the century, it was the much-maligned Art Nouveau —a style stemming directly from the Baroque and raised to exalted heights by the Catalán architect, Antonio Gaudí[66]— which, though indirectly and though foreign, directed the protests of the national esthetic background. The architect, Victor Dubugras, French also, turned to the tradition kept alive by native masonry masters to express the surging exuberance of the new style. . . . And on the wings

The Plaza of the Three Powers in Brasilia—one of the answers
to Lucio Costa's and Oscar Niemeyer's "search for new
and varied solutions . . ."

of the Art Nouveau, the esthetic protest soon took a turn towards a neo-colonial reaction "considered a definite return to the only true tradition."[67]

Reyner Banham points out with unquestionable accuracy that the group of contemporary architects in Brazil can be credited with having created the first national style of modern architecture —a style which "has been the envy of the world . . . and has kept the smooth surfaces —sometimes— and the simple geometry —when it feels like it— but it has carried them all to a degree of freedom so marked and so personal that the Italian critic Grillo Dorfles has, with some justification, termed it Neo-Baroque."[68]

Lúcio Costa alludes to Le Corbusier's pleas for "placing architecture beyond the utilitarian" but modestly does not reveal how instrumental he himself was in converting to reality this concept which has been of such basic importance in modern art history.[69] The seed sown by Le Corbusier was harvested in Brazil as it was no where else. Here the creator's dream was realized in the sense of restoring to architecture its primacy as leader of the fine arts, a position it had lost through the paralysis of the 19th century and had only begun to recuperate with the Art Nouveau.

In 1931 a group of enthusiastic architects[70] was formed in São Paulo to study and, where necessary, revise the fundamental work of Gropius, Mies Van der Rohe, Frank Lloyd Wright and the doctrines of Le Corbusier. From here arose the impulse which enabled Brazilian architects to proceed from theory to practice.

The first fruit was the Ministry of Education and Health, planned and built without the direct participation of Le Corbusier even though it was consonant with his principles and doctrines. As in the church in Pampulha (Minas Gerais) designed by Niemeyer,[71] the fusion of sculptural, architectural and pictorial values was once more linked with the baroque tradition of the unity of the arts.[72] Furthermore, decorative tile, as a genuine Portuguese-American contribution, incorporated or rather revived the plurality of this national art form, harmoniously present throughout the history of Brazilian art. Portinari joined the team

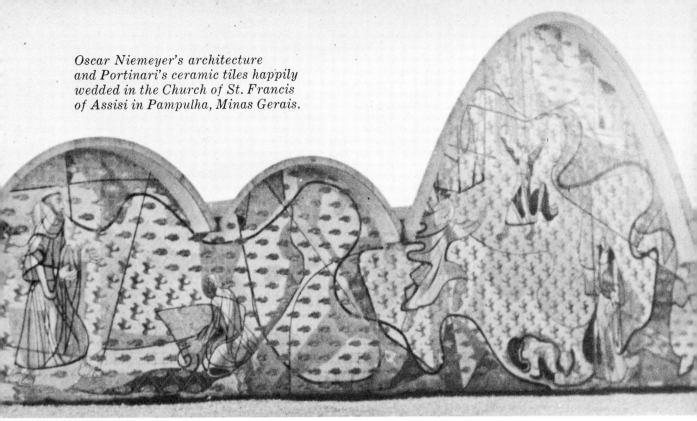

Oscar Niemeyer's architecture and Portinari's ceramic tiles happily wedded in the Church of St. Francis of Assisi in Pampulha, Minas Gerais.

The Ministry of Education and Health at Rio —first fruit of the "New Frontier" in architecture.

of architects and, voluntarily or not, the gifted painter with Niemeyer symbolized in our century the incomparable team of Aleijadinho and Mestre Ataíde.

Architecture's resumption of its rightful rank as leader of the fine arts was precisely the result of the equilibrium between the quality of construction and of plastic art which architecture shares or should share. Lúcio Costa concisely states the thesis when he defines it in terms of the problems the architect must solve within the margins defined by the calculations, the technique, the environment, the function and the program. Costa sustains that there can be no system other than that of appealing to the feelings in order to choose, from the scale of values lying within these extreme limits, the right plastic form for each detail in its indestructible relationship to the work as a unity.[73] (This is the same solution which Villa-Lobos, as we explained earlier,[26] applied to his neo-Bachian affiliation.)

The classico-baroque dualism stressed previously is expressed in Lúcio Costa's theory, on the one hand, "through the static conception of the form, in which the plastic energy contained in the object seems to develop from the outside toward the vital nucleus [predominance of the geometric volumes and continuity of the planes of definite contours] producing the sensation of equilibrium, of cohesion."[74] On the other hand, the energy concentrated in the object seems to want to free itself, an attitude Costa attributes to the spirit of Gothic in its resultant verticality and to the spirit of the Baroque in its simultaneous projection in opposing directions.

Perhaps this definition is the clearest expression of Niemeyer's aims when he explains, referring to Brasilia, that "Now in the three Palaces of the Uplands, Justice and the Dawn, I have restricted my speculations to the form of the supports or columns strictly so called. I did not want to adopt the usual sections —cylindrical or rectangular

The curved columns of the Palace of Justice frame
the administrative building of Congress in Brasilia.
Behind can be seen the white dome of the Senate.

Bruno Giorgi's
"Os Guerreiros"
(The Warriors)
echo the verticality
of the Congress
administrative
building towers
—another happy
marriage between
art and
architecture
in Brasilia.

The Congressional buildings in Brasilia: at left, the House of Representatives with its truncated sphere; at right, the domed Senate; in the center, the two soaring towers of the administrative building.

columns— which would have been simpler and cheaper, but sought other forms that, even though they might run counter to certain functionalist precepts, would give the buildings character, lightening them and creating an appearance of unattachment, as though they were merely resting on the ground. This justifies the forms adopted, with the ends tapering to a point, forms that greet the visitor with new and unexpected aspects; spreading out in a series of harmonious curves or, when he stands in the middle of the Plaza of the Three Powers, surrounding him —as Jean-Paul Sartre puts it— in the fan, as it were,

of their plastic interplay; or again changing and acquiring new and different aspects, as though they were not just things, inert and static."[75]

The principal challenge of modern architecture, particularly the Brazilian, to the practical and utilitarian bourgeois, is also deeply rooted in the esthetic past of the Ibero-American Baroque. The baroque architect, as we have seen, superimposed his ornamental imagination on the basic structures of the Renaissance.[76] The baroque characteristics of the open form, plastic expression striving for infinitude, grandeur as a legitimate function of the purpose of the work, are dazzlingly expressed in the Plaza of the Three Powers. No matter that the aims were achieved without the meticulous ornamental element typical of the Baroque. What is sure is that the Palace of the Congress was conceived in accordance with the interplay of the volumes and free spaces and, above all, visual depth and perspective.

It would not be too daring to relate the handling of the Plaza of the Three Powers to Bernini's solution for his immortal colonnade. It is not a question only of the esplanade which, as an integrated space, enhances the monumentality of the Plaza in Brasilia, but, as Niemeyer explains, the authority with which the domes characterize it —the exaltation of curved volumes, like the quintessence of the baroque infinitude, in balanced interplay between the truncated sphere and the infinite soaring verticality of the towers.

Richness and variety, also baroque attributes, link this conception with the architecture of Colonial Brazil, not through the simplified utilization of the elements of that epoch, but through the use of the same plastic purpose, the same love of the curve and the rich and refined forms that so well characterize it.

All these elements emphasize the feeling of virtually unlimited plastic freedom in revolt against functionalism or the tyranny of established techniques. Like Costa, Niemeyer and the newer Brazilian artists, we believe in the value of the imagination, in the new concepts capable of astonishing and moving because of what they contain of the creator, of freedom as the only source capable of creating ecstasy.

*Giorgi's Warriors stand guard
in the Plaza of the Three Powers
with the Palace of Justice
acting as a backdrop.*

The statue of
Blind Justice
keeps silent
vigil in front
of the Palace
of Justice in
Brasilia (photo
at far left)
From the statue
(photo at
immediate left)
across the wide
space of the
Plaza can be
seen the Palace
of the Planalto
and "the Warriors."

*The group of the "Official Theatres" clearly illustrates
the use of structural elements as ornamentation, a baroque
characteristic present in Brazil's modern architecture.*

The sloping, curved stairway
of the Palace of the Planalto
(photo above) is still another
striking example of the audacity
and freedom from the conventional
that characterizes both Brazil's
baroque and modern architecture.

In the photo at the left,
a window of the Palace of the
Planalto allows one to appreciate
the grandiose sweep of the
Plaza of the Three Powers.
At the right is the museum.

page 125

Bold and beautiful —the Cathedral at Brasilia.

the Baroque prevalence in Brazilian art

One of the Ministry buildings in Brasilia is seen from the interi
of the Cathedral (photo above). To the left is the dome of the Sena
At right, the soaring structures of the Cathedral "search for infinit

*A column of
the Cathedral:
an example of
Oscar Niemeyer's
"happy obsession
with the curve."*

Appendix

Notes

1 *Capoeira* is a popular gymnastic dance of both Negroes and mulattoes (it is sometimes danced, though much less gracefully, by whites) transplanted from Angola. Originally a struggle and triumphal dance, it became more strongly implanted in Bahia and Recôncavo than in the rest of the Brazilian littoral. Cf. Introduçao by José Geraldo Vieira to Kantor, Manuel: *Bahia*. Edições Melhoramentos, São Paulo, s.d.; Carneiro, E.: *Candomblés da Bahia*. Edit. Andes, Rio de Janeiro, 1954; Bastide, Roger: *Sociologia do Folcore Brasileiro*. Ed. Anhembí, São Paulo, 1959; Verger, P.: *Notes sur le culte des orisas et vodoun*, Memoires de l'Institut Français d'Afrique Noire. Dakar, 1957; Carybe: *Jogo da Capoeira*, Coleção Recôncavo, No. 3., Tipogr. Benedictina, Bahia, 1951.

2 *Jornal da Bahia,* 5/1/1961, 3rd caderno, p. 1.

3 Jewelers all over the world use this term and on the Isla de Margarita (Venezuela), an Elysian and legendary pearl-fishing center, the islanders use it constantly.

4 To clear up any confusion that may exist between the two concepts —Baroque and Rococo— it's best to note that the Rococo is a pseudo transitional style which should be differentiated from the Baroque. Actually, the Baroque and the Rococo should be considered in the history of style as almost antithetic concepts. Rococo is the mark of a brief transitional period between the Baroque and Neoclassicism with attributes from both styles. The derivation of the Rococo from the Baroque may be laid in good part to the forceful imposition of a French ideology on 18th century Europe. From the Baroque, the Rococo only retains

Notes

the apparent complexity and excessive ornamentation but —and this is what is most important —reduced to a minor tone, to the mere appearances. If the Baroque signifies strength, the Rococo signifies gallantry. The charming frivolity of the Rococo is antithetical to the dramatic passion of the Baroque. Both styles may, if you like, be considered unrestrained —but in opposite directions. Wyllie Sypher aptly summarizes the difference: "Rococo seems to be an anti-climax. Unlike Baroque, Rococo produced very little theory since its artists were inclined by temperament to be unacademic and unpedantic; they had a touch rather than a system." *(Rococo to Cubism in Art and Literature from the 18th to the 20th Century.* Vintage Books, New York, 1963, p. 4.) Cf. Hazard, Paul: *La Crise de la Conscience Européene,* 1935, ibid.: *La Pensée Européene au XVIIIème Siècle,* 1946; Kimball, Fiske: *The Creation of the Rococo,* 1943; Florisoone, Michel: *Le Dix-Huitième Siècle,* 1948.

5 Rêau, Louis: *Le Renaissance—L'Art Moderne,* Histoire Universelle des Arts, Vol. III, Chap. 3, Paris, 1936. Cf. Tapié, Victor-L.: *Baroque et Classicisme.* Paris, 1957. English translation, *The Age of Grandeur, Baroque Art and Architecture,* by A. Ross Williamson, F. A. Praeger, New York, 1961.

6 It is not within the purview of this essay to offer the reader an exhaustive analysis of the theories on the Baroque. We think it proper, however, to include here several ideas relating to the process of defining the Baroque.

The well-known categories of H. Wölfflin (see note 7), stemming from Riegl, constituted a new form of art history "without names" in contrast to the catalogue of works and biographies. The prevalence of the concept of style, with the necessary variants,

characterizes the bulk of the work printed after the appearance, early in the century, of the first works of Alois Riegl *(Die spaetro-emische Kunstindustrie im Zusammenhange mit der Gesamtentwicklung den bildenden Künste bei den Mittelmeervoelkern,* 1901; *Entstehung der Barockunst in Rom,* 1908. *Stilfragen,* 1893.) Wölfflin, favorite pupil of *Burckhardt (Die Kultur der Renaissance im Italien,* Stuttgart, 1860), outlined, with hitherto unsuspected projections, the new form of art history as a function of style with comparative omission of substantive evaluations. In addition to Wölfflin and others of less importance, Riegl's points of departure were amplified by: Dvorak *(Uber Kunstbetrachtung,* Munich, 1924; *Geschichte der italienischen Kunst im Zeitalter der Renaissance,* Munich, 1927), who makes them subordinate to the general history of ideas and, in particular, to philosophy and religion; Leo Balet *(Die Verbuergerlichung der deutschen Kunst, Literatur und Musik im 19 Jahrhundert,* Leipzig, 1936), who makes art conditional upon the intermingled action of all the historical domains, both material and ideological; W. Wörringer, disciple and critic of Riegl, who takes as his point of departure the concept of a history of the artistic will, ranging from his well-known *Abstraktion und Einfühlung* (Munich, 1908) up to *Fragen und Gegenfragen* (Munich, 1956); W. Hausenstein *(Von Geist der Barocks,* Munich, 1921); Eugenio d'Ors *(Teoría de los estilos y espejo de La Arquitetura,* Madrid, s.d.; ibid: *Lo Barroco,* Madrid, s.d.); W. Weisbach (see notes 48 and 49); J. Weingarten *(Der Geist des Barocks,* Augsburg, 1925).

7 Despite their repeated vulgarization, we consider it appropriate to summarize here Wölfflin's five well known categories for defining the Baroque as a contrast to certain ideals of the Renaissance: first, in contrast to the lineal concept, sensed by the hand, the pictorial concept, followed by the eye; second, in opposition to composition on a plane, composition in depth; third, in contradistinction to coordinated parts of equal value, parts subordinated to the whole; fourth, opposed to closed forms in which the observer is left outside, open forms which place the observer in their midst; fifth, in contrast to absolute clarity, relative clarity.

8 Cf. bibliography in note 6 as well as that of A. Ross Williamson, *op. cit.*

9 We believe it appropriate to credit once again as originator of the "theory of alternances" in the history of style this French essayist of the 19th century, ignored and almost forgotten by the majority of critics. Cf. Gebhardt, N.: *Les origines de la Renaissance en Italie.* Etudes Méridionales, Paris, 1887.

10 Cf. the studies on Albert Dührer in Hauser, Arnold: *The Social History of Art.* Vintage Books, New York, 1960.

11 W. Worringer, in commenting on Schmarsow's formula —"Art is man's meeting with nature"— adds: "Still to be written is a psychology of the artistic necessity —or, using a term consonant with our modern viewpoint— a psychology of the stylistic necessity. It would be a history of the vital feeling and as such would take its place, as a science of equal rank, alongside the history of religions. By vital feeling I mean the psychic state in which humanity finds itself in each case when faced by the cosmos, by the phenomena of the external world. This state is manifested in the quality of the psychic necessities, in other words, in the constitution of absolute artistic will, and finds its external expression in the work of art, that is, in the

style of this work, whose individuality is precisely the same individuality as that of the psychic necessities. It is in this way that the stylistic evolution of art among the various peoples reveals, exactly as does its theogony, the different levels of what we call the vital feeling." (*Abstraktion und Einfühlung,* op cit., p. 38.)

12 Suffice it to single out a number of well-known events to prove the validity of this contention. In Spain, Germany and even in Flanders, the transition from the late Gothic (which Wörringer and Henri Focillon, *Art d'Occident,* Paris 1938, pp. 293 *et seq.,* called "baroquized") to the early Baroque took place almost without a break in continuity. Hieronymus Bosch and Grünewald are contemporaries of Leonardo, Rafael and Botticelli. The Hispanicism of Boscán and Garcilaso is highly debatable, particularly if compared to that of Góngora and Quevedo. The famous façade of Tomar dates from the mid-16th century.

13 Cf. the statement of Albert Camus in the preface to *L'Envers et L'Endroit,* Paris 1958, as quoted by Papadaki, Stamo: *Oscar Niemeyer,* George Braziller, New York, 1960, p. 7: "A great many injustices occur in this world, but there is one that nobody mentions, the injustice of climate."

14 See the list of 37 monographs and other works of research and analysis by Prof. Robert C. Smith on the art of Brazil in the introduction by José Valladares to Prof. Smith's *Arquitetura Colonial: As Artes na Bahia,* I Parte. Livraria Progresso Editora, Salvador, 1955. Prof. Robert C. Smith is considered the greatest American authority on Brazilian art. He has been enormously instrumental in diffusing knowledge on colonial art since before his work with the His-

Notes

panic Foundation of the Library of Congress up to the present as faculty member of the University of Pennsylvania.

15 Cf. especially Buschiazzo, Mario J.: *Historia de la Arquitectura Colonial en Iberoamérica.* Emecé Editores, Buenos Aires, 1961. Cf. also the similar studies by Mr. and Mrs. Meza-Gisbert in AIAAIE (Vol. 7, 1954, p. 3 *et seq.*) of Buenos Aires. See acronyms following bibliography.)

16 For a commented bibliography of the subject see Damaz, Paul: *Art in European Architecture.* Reinhold, New York, 1956; Castedo, L.: *En torno a los valores del estilo. Corrientes actuales acerca de la unidad de forma y expresión en música, pintura, escultura arquitectura, poesía, drama, danza.* RMCh XLI (Autumn) 1951.

17 The painters of the Gupta period in India (4th to 6th century A.D.) derived their art from the dance. (See Sachs, Curt: *The Commonwealth of Art: Style in Fine Arts, Music and Dance.* W. W. Norton & Co., New York, 1946.) Vitruvius suggested to Roman architects that they familiarize themselves with melody and rhythm. Goethe defined the sensory equivalences, the taste of colors —the alkaline taste of blue, the acid taste of yellow, the "antwortende Gegenbilder." (Cf. Müller, Günther: *Die Gestaltfrage in der Literaturwissenschaft und Goethes Morphologie.* Max Niemeyer Publ., Halle, a.S., 1944.) Schlegel found "continuous communications between the arts. Columns can become pictures, pictures poems, poems music, and religious music would arise like a temple in the air." (Cf. the analysis in Focillon, Henri: *The Life of Forms in Arts* (translation). Hogan & Kubler, New York, 1948.) Rimbaud gave universal form to the synethesia in his celebrated sonnet and, by attributing color to the vowels, launched the dogmas of poetic symbolism. Baudelaire *(Curiosités esthétiques)* sang: "Les parfumes, les couleurs et les sons se répondent." (Cf. Souza, R. de: *Le Rythme poétique.* Paris, 1892; Léauteaud, J.: *Symbolisme litteraire.* Lyon, 1901.) The kinship between the "Fêtes galantes" and the "Suite Bergamasque" is absolute. Verlaine and Debussy coincide with different means of expression in the same stylistic body of ideas. Examples could be given *ad infinitum*. It should be noted, however, that the historians we have cited have dispensed with the Hellenic unity of the fine arts, maintaining these separate and as though in water-tight compartments. In many countries a traditional dividing line is drawn in speaking of art and architecture as if architecture were not an art. Because of a very curious phenomenon, the search for a historical approach to this unity has so far always been launched by the musicologists and literary historians. This is perhaps because the concept of style is more easily applicable to these two disciplines. Or perhaps because, according to Hans Seldmayr, style is more a matter of form than of content. Be that as it may, we are indebted to Hugo Leichtentritt, Curt Sachs and P. Lang for the terminology currently used today, and to Valdemar Vedel, Ludwig Pfandl and Karl Wossler for the stylistic analysis of the literary work reflecting similar expressions of the other fine arts. Cf., with reference to Spanish America, Henríquez Ureña, Pedro: *Las Corrientes Literarias en la América Hispana.* Fondo de Cultura Económica, México, 1948; Picón Salas, Mariano: *Barroco de Indias* in *De la Conquista a la Independencia.* Fondo de Cultura Económica, México, 1956; Damaz, Paul F.: *Art in Latin American Architecture.* Preface by Oscar Niemeyer. Reinhold, New York, 1963.

18 For the literary analysis, cf. the recent critical works of Afranio Coutinho. For the baroque root, cf. the work by the same author: *Aspectos da Literatura Barroca.* Rio de Janeiro, 1950. See also the works of Rodolfo Teofilo, Fernando Azevedo, Paulo Prado, Garciliano Ramos, Raquel de Queiroz, José Luis do Rego, Lúcio Cardosa, José Americo de Almeyda.

19 Let us note in passing that the meeting of the historic event with the artistic expression is reinforced in Brazil by the tropical culture in a fashion very similar to that of India. See Freyre, Gilberto: *Arte, Ciência e Trópico.* São Paulo, 1962.

20 Vignola's Church of the Gesú —the point of departure for students of what was later to be called by some scholars the "Jesuit style"— still retains tympans and pediments and is based on the basilican plan. These features, however, in later examples, were soon to be broken up and the extremities were to become coiled in complicated convolutions and volutes which were increasingly exaggerated as time passed and the style reached its zenith. Nonetheless, the Greco-Roman formal substratum was to persist. As a consequence, upon the static base of classicism was superimposed the dynamics of a movement culminating in a new spatial feeling —from Bernini and Borromini all the way to the Bavarian, Hungarian and Bohemian extremes.

21 The Plateresque represents, in our eyes, a symbol of Ibero and Ibero-American resistance to the universal patterns of a re-awakening classicism. If the thesis that Spain passed through the Renaissance without assimilating it is valid, this is best demonstrated in her plateresque architecture and sculpture. The term "plateresque" came into existence in Spain during the 16th century.

Lope de Vega calls the masons of Madrid *"plateros del yeso"*—silversmiths in plaster— a term which Menéndez y Pelayo considers a happy choice. Without pretending to define summarily such a complex style, let us at least clarify that, during the first half of the 16th century, the Plateresque imposed on Gothic and classic structural elements a layer of gold and silver work of predominantly Moorish design on the Italian forms. Of great interest, but which can be mentioned only in passing in a work of this scope, are the functional modifications which the Latin American environment imposed upon the Plateresque, especially in Mexico. The Plateresque dominates the reign of Charles V and is a direct descendant of the Isabelin and Manuelin in Portugal. Cf. in addition to the bibliography at the end, Camón Aznar, José: *La Arquitectura Plateresca.* Consejo Superior de Investigaciones Científicas, Instituto Diego Velásquez, Madrid, 1945 (which has an extensive bibliography); Mac Gregor, Luis: *El Plateresco en México,* Editorial Porrúa, México, 1954.

22 The repetition of the architectonic and ornamental outline of the high altar on the stone of the façade is called *fachada-retablo.* Cf. particularly Buschiazzo and Toussaint in the bibliography.

23 Cf. Buschiazzo, *op. cit.,* as well as the collaboration of this author with Diego Angulo Iñiguez and Enrique Marco Dorta in *Historia del Arte Hispanoamericano,* cited in the bibliography. See also Bazin, Germain: *L'Architecture religieuse baroque au Brésil.* Museu de Arte, São Paulo/Editions d'Histoire et d'Art, Librairie Plon, Paris, 1957.

24 Quoted from the Spanish translation of the German *Space in Baroque Architecture* by

Notes

the architects Joaquín Rodríquez Saumell and Patricio H. Randle for AIAAIE, University of Buenos Aires, 9, 1956, pp. 53-69.

25 Alain Resnais has succeeded in giving plastic form to this expression through the medium of the cinema. It is not by chance, moreover, that a baroque Central European mansion was chosen as the setting for "Last Year in Marienbad." The conscious play between yesterday, today and tomorrow; the symbolism of a dynamic statue which the camera renders even more serpentine; the concentration on and displacement toward detail; the plastic category of shadow —all are so many baroque elements which the creator links together in his film to place it beyond time.

26 The study of this volitional kinship and the stylistic coincidences would be suitable material for a fascinating work. Suffice it to point out the ideological parallel and similarity of construction between the Bachiana No. 5 for soprano and cellos and the air for contralto and violin obligato in the Agnus Dei of the B Minor Mass of Bach. The system proposed by Souriau (*La Correspondence des Arts. Eléments d'Esthétique comparée.* Librairie Plon, Paris, 1947), of studying morphology by expressing the musical "lines" through trigonometric means, would in both cases give figures of extraordinary similarity.

27 The implications of the concept are clear in Wörringer (*Abstraktion and Einfühlung, op. cit.,* p. 59): "The oscillations of the state of mind are reflected . . . in parallel fashion in the religious conceptions and the artistic volition of a people. It is thus that the waning of the cosmic instinct, as it contents itself with an external orientation in the universal panorama, always coincides with a waxing of the longing for a sentimental projection, existing in latent form in every human being, and is repressed only by agoraphobia, by the longing for abstraction. That is when it begins to come alive in the external world, thanks to man, from whom it receives all of its life, which anthropomorphizes his entire being, all his innermost forces."

28 The nationality of Hamlet is fortuitous and circumstantial; he could have been born either in Denmark or Poland without its making much difference. Conversely, Don Juan is Sevillian and Don Quixote could only come from La Mancha. The subject is tempting. The distinctive and exclusive nature of Dostoevsky's personages, which could only be Russian, would go to prove once more, according to the preceding hypothesis, the psychological identity between Slavs and Iberians, a theme fully developed by a number of scholars. Shakespeare situates his characters in Italy, Egypt or Denmark surely because his desire for universality so impelled him. The same might be said of Goethe, Voltaire or Hemingway. Conversely, the archetype of the Commander whom Lope de Vega invented could function only in Fuenteovejuna, Lazarillo in Tormes and Quixote in Toboso. Applying this thesis to Lusitanian culture, the proof can be found by comparing the Iliad to the Lusiads.

29 Up to the close of the 17th century, the Portuguese devoted themselves in their American colony to the cultivation of the land and the extraction of Brazil wood because "no mines could be found. . . ." In 1695, the first news reached São Paulo and the coastal cities of a fabulous discovery. In the hinterland there were enormous quantitites of gold. Poor and rich alike abandoned their businesses, homes, families. The Capitanîas began to become depopulated, agriculture to decline and sugar mills to fail. Shortly after the *bandeirantes,* still other people from Europe —the Portuguese and Spanish particularly— arrived. As in all gold rushes, the social climate was one of extreme violence. In the mid-18th century, the first signs that the mines were exhausted heightened the unrest. The uprisings against the allocations of taxes to complete the *quintos* culminated in the *Inconfidência* captained by Tiradentes. It was quelled in a bloodbath but the germ of revolt remained alive in Brazil. In this atmosphere and this climate the initial creative phase of Aleijadinho unfolded.

30 Bretas, Rodrigo José Ferreira: *Traços biográphicos relativos ao finado Antônio Francisco Lisboa, distincto esculptor mineiro, mais conhecido pelo apellido de Aleijadinho.* Correo Official de Minas, Nos. 169 and 170, 1858.

31 With great perspicacity, the Brazilian Government long since declared Ouro Preto (the city of Aleijadinho) to be a national monument. Preserved in it is the bulk of his work which has been studied and documented by the technicians of the SPHAN (Serviço do Patrimonio Histórico e Artîstico Nacional) and particularly by its director, Rodrigo M. F. de Andrade, by Antonio Joaquim de Almeida, director of the Museu de Ouro in Sabará, by Germain Bazin in his most recent book on Aleijadinho (*Aleijadinho et la Sculpture baroque au Brésil,* Le Temps, Paris, 1963) and by numerous other savants from America and Europe.

32 For Aleijadinho's physical aspect cf. Penalva, Gastão: *Iconografia do Aleijadinho,*

en Espello, Rio de Janeiro, Marzo, 1955; in addition see Bazin's commentary and interpretation in *Aleijadinho et la Sculpture baroque au Brésil, op. cit.,* p. 91.

33 Bazin, *op. cit.* pp. 97-98, analyses five interpretations of Aleijadinho's illness: 1.) syphilis, which in its tertiary effects can produce necrosis of the extremities; 2.) the "zamparina" already described; 3.) the "cardina," a horrible effect produced by erotic drugs; 4.) crippling rheumatoid arthritis, the same disease that rendered Renoir's hand useless; 5.) leprosy, discarded by Bazin for previously explained reasons.

34 Six travelers refer in their descriptions of Brazil to the loss or ankylosis of Aleijadinho's hands: Wilhelm Eschwege, John Luccoc, A. de Saint Hilaire, Friedrich von Woech, Francis de Castelnau and Richard F. Burton. Cf. the bibliography and commentaries in Bazin's *op. cit.,* p. 97 and notes.

35 Reis, José de Sousa: *O Adro do Santuário de Congonhas.* Revue of SPHAN, No. 3, 1939, pp. 207-226.

36 With sound reasoning Hans Mann (The 12 Prophets of Antônio Francisco Lisboa, "O Aleijadinho." Ministerio de Educação e Cultura, Serviço de Documentação, Rio de Janeiro, 1958) supposes that at some time an exchange was made in the location of the statues of Jonah and Joel. Actually the Biblical chronology is restored if their places are exchanged. Furthermore —and we believe that this argument based on composition is more valid than the one above— there can be discerned in the orientation of the statues a premeditated effort to focus the torsos toward the axis of sight of the spectator if the latter is standing before the staircase. At present, Jonah and Joel have their torso and face turned outward from the composition.

37 Cf. particularly Felipe, Léon: *Jonás se equivoca. Obras completas.* Losada, Buenos Aires, 1963. Both the Prophets and the Stations of the Cross invite a comparison of Aleijadinho's capacity for expressiveness with the musical symbolism that Albert Schweitzer develops in his *Bach, le musicien poète*. In Jeremiah's prophecy the text reads: "Behold I send a multitude of fishers, saith the Eternal, and they shall fish; and after this I shall send a multitude of hunters and they shall hunt." In Bach's Cantata No. 38, *"Siehe, ich will viel Fischer aussenden,"* the music of the first section describes the movement in the empty spaces, since the word "fisher" evokes in Bach the idea of a lake; in the second section (Allegro cuasi presto), the hunters course over the mountain and fanfares are heard. There is another profound relationship between the expression of arrogance within the contrition Aleijadinho confers on his Jonah and the same idea expressed by Bach in his Cantata No. 176, *"Es ist ein trotzig un versagtes Ding."* An exhaustive study by the Bachgesellschaft, completing the work of Charles Vidor and Albert Schweitzer, makes it possible to arrive at a parallel interpretation in sculpture and in music of the biblical text by these two geniuses of the Baroque who surely could never have known anything at all of one another.

38 *América en la Historia.* Fondo de Cultura Económico, Mexico, 1959, p. 237.

39 *Casa grande e Senzala* (Formação da familia Brasileira sob o regime de economia patriarchal). Livraria José Olimpo, Rio de Janeiro, 2nd ed., 1951, p. 128.

40 *Charango,* a popular instrument among the mestizos of the Peruvian-Bolivian plateau, is a small four-string (sometime doubled) guitar whose sounding box is made from the shell of a *quirquincho* or armadillo.

41 The Ibero-American identification can be verified by a comparative analysis of the Last Suppers of Aleijadinho and Salzillo, the latter in the Ermita de Jesús in Murcia, Spain. Both groups exhibit in common the eloquence of the hands. "As they did eat, He said to them: verily I say unto you, that one of you shall betray Me. And they were exceedingly sorrowful and began every one of them to say unto Him, Lord, is it I?" (Matthew, 26, 21-22) All the apostles protest with a gesture and with a movement of the hands —all, except Judas Iscariot. The similarity between the sculptural expression and choreography of Aleijadinho's work, expressed in the same manner though at immeasurable geographical and relational distances from Salzillo, further enhances the resemblance in which any possibility of influence is entirely out of the question. The differences arise in terms of the universality previously mentioned. Salzillo's Christ is a Murcian peasant. Aleijadinho's is an elegant European with Oriental eyes. In Salzillo's creation, the hands move in a single plane about 8 inches from the table. In Aleijadinho's, they gesticulate, protest angrily, rise and fall, forming a true, irregular Grecian fret. Both masterpieces once again point up the danger in speaking of "influence" when frequently it is merely a question of coincidence. (See Wörringer, *Abstraktion und Einfünlung, op cit.* pp. ii, 4.) In making this observation, we have in mind a number of works dealing with Aleijadinho. Leon Kochnitzky in "Black Gold of Brazil's Baroque" *(Art News,* New York, Jan. 15, 1942) says: "Except for a few illustrated Dutch or German editions of the Bible, he [Aleijadinho] had little contact with European art." With respect to the Dutch Bibles, we greatly share in this suspicion. But where are these Bibles? What years and what editions are meant? Who were the engravers? (Cf. the study of the 15th century Florentine etchings of the Prophets and their likeness to Aleijadinho's in Bazin, *Aleijadinho et la Sculpture baroque au Brésil, op. cit.,* pp. 271 & 273.) A like observation can be made about Chapter ii in the recent work by Padre Heliodoro Pires *(Mestre Aleijadinho. Vida e obra de Antônio Francisco Lisboa, Gigante da Arte no Brasil.* Nacional Edit., Rio de Janeiro, 1961) in which he atempts to establish a relationship between the cartouches of the Prophets and those of the Cathedral of Amiens. Regarding the inconography of The Last Supper, see in particular plates 66 to 71, 85, 88, 89, 92 to 99, 101 to 104, 106 to 112, 115 to 117, 127, 128, 135, 141 to 143, 145, 146 and 155 in Bagué, Enrique and Petit, Juan: *La Eucaristía.* Edit. Seix Barralt, Barcelona, 1952. Of Salzillo's "Figures for the Last Supper" (Murcia, Church of Jesús), the commentators say: "It is one of the most justly renowned works by its author, from the period between 1745 and 1765, when the artist, born in 1701, had already reached his maturity, but had not yet fallen into the facile, over-sentimental affectedness which characterized his production in later years." Cf. also Lafaye, J. and Bottineau, V. Y.: *Spanien, Schönheiten und Schätze,* Droemer-Knaur, München, 1962, with excellent photographs of Salzillo's Last Supper; Subias G., Juan: *El Arte Popular en España,* Seix Barralt, Barcelona, 1948; Pantorba, Bernardino de: *Imagineros Españoles.* Ed. Mayfee, Madrid, 1952.

42 See particularly Andrade, Rodrigo M. F. de: *Contribuição para o estudo da obra do Aleijadinho.* SPHAN No. 2, 1938; SPHAN No. 15, 1951; the *op. cit.* of José de Sousa Reis; Martins, Judith: *Apontamentos para a biographia de Antônio Francisco Lisboa.* SPHAN No. 3, 1939. Of great merit are the analyses of Robert C. Smith in his extensive works (over 40 publications on Brazilian art). See also the opinion of Martin Soria in Kubler and Soria: *Art and Architecture in Spain and Portugal and their American Dominions.* The Pelican History of Art, Penguin Books, Suffolk-Bradford, 1959. (The special bibliography on Aleijadinho is very abundant and, generally, more literary than scientific.)

43 *Op. cit.*

44 Mariano Filho, José: *Antônio Francisco Lisboa, O Aleijadinho.* Rio de Janeiro, 1944; *ibid: Antônio Francisco Lisboa, O Estatuario.* Mensario do Jornal do Comércio, Tome 9, Vol. 1, January 1940; *ibid:* Os Mistérios da Arte de Antônio Francisco Lisboa. Mensario do Jornal do Comércio, Tome 8, Vol. 3, 1945. See also Bazin's commendatory opinion in the bibliography of his *op cit.* with regard to José Mariano Filho.

45 Machado, Lourival Gomes: *Reconquista de Congonhas.* Photographs by Eduardo Ayrosa. Instituto Nacional do Livro, Rio de Janeiro, 1960.

46 According to Condillac's philosophy, "There is nothing in the mind which was not first in the senses."

47 We set no great store in defense of our thesis in the literature on eroticism —especially on the French and German literature, as abundant as it is pornographic in general. (See especially, Bataille, G.: *Les*

Notes

larmes d'Eros. Paris, 1961, and Sorel, J.: *L'Erotisme de la Bible*. Paris, 1962, in the *Bibliothèque Internationale d'Erotologie*, Jean Jacques Pauvert, Editeur. For the same reason we have paid even less heed to the purely psychoanalytical interpretations which usually find the rose erotic and consider sexual whatever is seen by the eye or palpable to the touch. Suffice it to recall the Freudian version of weaving. Cf. Garma, Angel: *Psicoanálisis del Arte Ornamental*. Ed. Paidos, Buenos Aires, 1961; *Art and Psychoanalysis*. Ed. by William Phillips, Meridian Books, Cleveland, 1963 (with many references and bibliography).

48 Weisbach, Werner: *Der Barock als Kunst der Gegenreformation*. Berlin, 1921. Quotations from the Spanish ed.: *El Barroco, Arte de la Contrarreforma*. Translation and introductory essay by Enrique Lafuente Ferrari, 2nd ed., Espasa-Calpe, Madrid, 1948.

49 In the Spanish edition of Weisbach's *op. cit.*, the translator, Enrique Lafuente Ferrari, soundly analyzes this resistance to sensual expression in Spanish art although limiting it to the nude —in other words, to its implicit sexual expression, always so difficult for the Peninsular. Professor Lafuente Ferrari maintains (with his extensive published works and teaching experience) that Spain never warmed to the "tolerances" that were introduced in Italy or Flanders after Trent. "There are no Furinis in the art of Spain." He cites as examples the Magdalene and Saint Agnes of Ribera. On this subject and many others treated in this work, see Ferguson's classic *Signs and Symbols in Christian Art*, Hesperides Books, London, 1954.

50 Westheim, Paul: *Arte Antiguo de México* Fondo de Cultra Económica, México, 1950. See in particular Part I, Chap. 4.

51 We note these sporadic examples without dwelling on the relationship established by psychologists between the erotic and death. In this connection, we could project the Mexican form of sensuality onto the dual Hispano-Indian manner of artistically portraying death. Cf. Moreno Villa, José: *Lo Méxicano*. El Colegio de México, México, 1948.

52 This phenomenon raises the problem of two fascinating unknowns: the first rests on the rupture between the Castilian ornamental asceticism added to the chastity of the Indian and the numerous erotic examples to be found in pre-Hispanic pottery, as well as in the phallic musical instruments patiently collected by Traversari in the Casa de la Cultura Ecuatoriana in Quito. The second unknown, which might well explain the loss of sensory and pantheistic quality in Hispano-American art, lies in the mysterious proliferation of tropical animal and vegetable ornamentation on the *altiplano* (highlands). Cf. Buschiazzo, Mario J.: *La Arquitectura de las Misiones de Moxos y Chiquitos*. Separata of *Südamerika* (Buenos Aires) Year IV, No. 3, Nov.-Dec. 1953.

53 On the other hand, the basic value of Brazilian sensuality transferred to art represents a corroboration of one of the most lucid chapters in the work of Wörringer, *op cit.*, p. 61 *et seq*. "It is obvious that desire for sentimental expression can only arise where, owing to the predisposition, the development, favorable climatic conditions and other propitious assumptions, a certain relation of trust has arisen between man and the world about him. In such conditions, the sensual security, the blind trust in the surrounding world, the elimination of speculation, the sense of well-being in this world lead, in the field of religion, to a pantheism —or polytheism in certain cases— that is ingeniously anthropomorphic; in the artistic field, to a felicitous naturalism, a joyous devotion to the mundane. . . . There are men . . . for whom, so strong is their faith in the reality of existence, so too, is their faith in understanding that it serves to orient them outwardly in the world."

54 In 1733, a procession was held in Minas Gerais with the most heterogeneous mixture imaginable of Christian and pagan symbols. The allegorical themes were: "The serpent of Eden, the moon surrounded by nymphs. Negroes and mulattoes spiritedly danced their orgiastic heathen dances in honor of the Saviour and the Saints." (Compare this description by a German traveler with the austerity of gesture and movement of the Bolivian *Diablada.)*

55 Germain Bazin, studying the carvings in Minas Gerais, agrees with this idea. *op. cit.,* 1, 309.

56 *Arte, Ciência e Trópico,* op. cit., pp. 111-112.

57 *Ibid:* p. 105.

58 Bruno, Ernani Silva: *Imagens da formação do Brasil.* Ed. Cultrix, São Paulo, 1962. The examples of syncretism could be extended indefinitely, e.g., the African Catholic Masses extremely well known from commercial records.

59 *Op. cit.,* Tome 1, pp. 271 *et seq.* Cf. Kubler and Soria, *op. cit.* p. 192; Milne, James Lees: *Baroque in Spain and Portugal.* London, 1960; especially, Smith, Robert C.: *op. cit.,* pp. 54-55.

60 *Op. cit.* p. 60.

61 Compare with the angels of the frieze of the Cantoria by the sensual Donatello in Florence.

62 In the turgescences of Baroque painting and sculpture, one frequently encounters expressions of erotic sensualism, above all in the works dealing with mythological themes. However, rarely is this type of sensualism incorporated in religious art. André Malraux discovered some examples in his "Musée Imaginaire de la Sculpture Mondiale." Cf. *Le Monde Chrétien,* Gallimard, Paris, 1954, especially plates 11, 13, 32, 51, 68, 80, 98, 121, 190 and 201.

63 Costa, Lúcio: *Sôbre Arquitetura.* Volume I, Centro dos Estudantes universitários de Arquitetura, Facultade de Arquitetura da Universidade do Rio Grande do Sul, Pôrto Alegre, 1962. (A compilation of articles and essays by the master architect, reprinted without his authority.)

64 Quotation from the contribution, "Brazil," by Henrique E. Mindlin for the *Encyclopaedia of Modern Architecture.* Gerd Hatje, gen. ed. Thames & Hudson, London, 1963.

65 Henrique E. Mindlin, one of the leaders among Brazil's group of new architects and designer of the well-known Avenida Central Building in Rio de Janeiro (1961), has an excellent summary of this period in his book, *L'Architecture Moderne au Brésil,* Colibris Ed., Rio de Janeiro/Amsterdam, 1956. Cf. also Barata, Mário: *A Arquitetura Brasileira dos Séculos XIX e XX.* Separata de *"Aspectos da Formação e Evolução do Brasil,* Jornal do Comércio, Rio de Janeiro, 1952; Machado, Lourival Gomes: *Retrato da Arte Moderna do Brasil.* Gráfica de Prefeitura, São Paulo, 1948 (a special study of the "Semana da Arte Moderna").

66 For the last few decades, critics have considered Gaudí as a "master of world archi-

Notes

tecture. Although a medievalist by inclination, the Catalán architect was non-traditional in his invention of forms and about 1900 became closely associated with the prevalent Art Nouveau style in Catalonia. By 1910 his increasing preoccupation with the *Sagrada Familia* Church, of which he had long been the architect, led him to relinquish all his secular projects for ecclesiastical building." Collins, George R.: *Antonio Gaudí*. Braziller, New York, 1960.

67 Mindlin, Henrique: *op. cit.*, p. 3.

68 Banham, Reyner: *Guide to Modern Architecture*. Architectural Press, London, 1962, p. 63.

69 In January of 1964 we visited Lúcio Costa in his small office at the Serviço do Patrimônio where the architect dedicates a good part of his creative capacity to the study and evaluation of Brazil's colonial art. During our long and rewarding conversation with him, on our request, he enlarged upon his ideas regarding the static and dynamic styles which he had so ably developed in his *Consideraçoes sôbre arte contemporánea*. He demonstrated, with arguments which we have attempted to incorporate in this essay, the importance of the new Brazilian architecture as the principle motivating force behind the aforementioned plastic quality and lyric and emotional content of the architectonic work. These qualities, according to Lúcio Costa, will cause the architectural work to survive after it no longer has a functional reason for being.

70 The team formed to achieve the project consisted of Lúcio Costa, Oscar Niemeyer, Jorge Machado Moreira, Alfonso Eduardo Reydi, Ernani Vasconcelos and Carlos Leão.

71 Cf. Papadaki, Stamo: *The Work of Oscar Niemeyer*. Reinhold, New York, 1950; *Ibid.: Oscar Niemeyer; Works in Progress*. Reinhold, New York, 1956; *Ibid: Oscar Niemeyer*. Braziller, New York, 1960.

72 Damaz, Paul: *Art in Latin American Architecture*. Reinhold, New York, 1963. See especially Part 1: Brasil, Portinari, Burle Marx and the Brazilian Azulejos, pp. 68-107.

73 Cf. Costa, Lúcio: *Considerações sôbre Arte Contemporánea*. Os Cadernos de Cultura del SDMEC, No. 6. Quotation from *ibid:* p. 203.

74 *Op. cit.*, p. 205.

75 *Módulo*. Revista de Arquitetura e artes visuais do Brasil. Rio de Janeiro, Vol. 4, No. 21. diciembre de 1960, pp. 1-7.

76 Papadaki, Stamo: *op. cit.* See especially Chap. 3, "The Case of a Lyric Architecture," pp. 25-32.

Bibliography

General Documents

Buschiazzo, Mario J.: *Bibliografía de Arte Colonial Argentino*. Universidad de Buenos Aires, IAAIE, Buenos Aires, 1947.
  Documentos de Arte Colonial Sudamericano. Publ. de la Academia Nacional de Bellas Artes de la República Argentina. Buenos Aires, 1943-1956.

Dorta, Enrique Marco: *Fuentes para la Historia del Arte Hispanoamericano, Estudios y Documentos*. Instituto Diego Velázquez, Sevilla, 1960.

Hanson, Earl Parker, (ed.): *New World Guides to the Latin American Republics,* New York, 1945.

Smith, Robert C. and Wilder, Elizabeth: *A Guide to Latin American Art*. Hispanic Foundation, The Library of Congress, Washington, 1948.

Valladares, José: *Arte Brasileira*. Publicações de 1943-1953, bibliografia comentada com índice remissivo. Livraria Progresso Ed., Salvador, Bahia, 1955.
  Arte Brasileira. Publicações de 1954, bibliografia comentada com índice remissivo. Livraria Progresso Ed., Salvador, Bahia, 1958.

Vargas Ugarte, Rubén S.J.: *Ensayo de un Diccionario de Artífices coloniales de la América meridional*. Talleres gráficos A. Baiocco, Lima, 1947.

Latin America

Angulo Iñiguez, Diego, Dorta, Enrique Marco and Buschiazzo, Mario J.: *Historia del Arte Hispanoamericano*. Salvat, Barcelona, 1945-56.

Banham, Reyner: *Guide to Modern Architecture*. Architectural Press, London, 1962.

Buschiazzo, Mario J.: *Estudios de Arquitectura*

Bibliography

Colonial Hispanoamericana. Ed. Guillermo Kraft, Buenos Aires, 1944.

Historia de la Arquitectura Colonial en Ibero-américa. Emecé, Buenos Aires, 1961.

Cali, François, Arthaud, Claude and Hébert-Stevens, François: *L'Art des Conquistadors.* Arthaud, Paris, 1960.

Damaz, Paul F.: *Art in Latin American Architecture.* Preface by Oscar Niemeyer. Reinhold, New York, 1963.

Dony, Paul: *Kirchliche Barockarchitektur in Portugal, Bayern und Brasilien.* "Das Münster," 10th year, Jan.-Feb., 1957.

Lateinamerikanische Jesuitenkirchen. Kollegienkirchen. "Das Münster." 12th year, Jan.-Feb., 1959.

Géo-Charles: *Art baroque en Amérique Latine.* Plon, Paris, 1954.

Kelemen, Pál: *Baroque and Rococo in Latin America.* Macmillan, New York, 1951.

Kubler, George and Soria, Martín: *Art and Architecture in Spain and Portugal and their American Dominions, 1500 to 1800.* The Pelican History of Art, Penguin Books, Suffolk-Bradford, 1959.

Noel, Martín S.: *El Arte en la América Española.* Institución Cultural Española, Buenos Aires, 1942.

Estudios y Documentos para la Historia del Arte Colonial. Arquitectura Virreinal. Instituto de Investigaciones Históricas de la Facultad de Filosofía y Letras. Universidad de Buenos Aires, Buenos Aires, 1934.

Sartorio, Alberto: *Encyclopédie de l'Architecture Moderne:* Ordre et Climat Américain, Milan, 1954.

Solá, Miguel: *Historia del Arte Hispanoamericano.* Ed. Labor, Barcelona, 1958.

Torre Revello, José: *Estudios y Documentos para la Historia del Arte Colonial.* Tome II, Instituto de Investigaciones Históricas de la Facultad de Filosofía y Letras, Universidad de Buenos Aires, Buenos Aires, 1944.

Brazil

Andrade, Rodrigo M. F. de: *As Artes Plásticas no Brasil.* Vol. I, Sul América e Banco Hipotecário, Rio de Janeiro, 1952.

As Artes Plásticas no Brasil. Vol. I, Ethnografia Nacional ed., Rio de Janeiro, 1962.

Azevedo, Fernando de: *A Cultura Artística.* In "Cultura Brasileira," Instituto Brasileiro de Geografia Estatística, Vol. I, Rio de Janeiro, 1943.

Bandeira, Manuel: *Guide d'Ouro Preto.* Trans. and notes by Michel Simon. Ministério de Relações Exteriores, Rio de Janeiro, 1948.

Barata, Mário: *A Arquitetura Brasileira dos Séculos XIX e XX.* Separata de "Aspectos da Formação e Evolução do Brasil," Jornal do Comércio, Rio de Janeiro, 1952.

Panorama da Arte Moderna no Brasil. In "Arquitetura contemporânea," Rio de Janeiro, No. 1, Aug.-Sept., 1953.

Bazin, Germain: *Aleijadinho et la Sculpture baroque au Brésil.* Le Temps, Paris, 1963.

L'Architecture religieuse au Brésil. Museu de Arte, São Paulo / Plon, Paris, 1956-1957.

Bergen, E.: *Oscar Niemeyer. In* "Bouwen en Wonen," Antwerp, Jan., 1957.

Bretas, Rodrigo José Ferreira: *Traços biográphicos relativos ao finado Antônio Francisco Lisboa, distincto esculptor mineiro, mais conhecido pelo apellido de Aleijadinho.* Correo Official de Minas. Nos. 169 and 170, 1858.

Bury, John: *Estilo Aleijadinho and the Churches of Eighteenth Century Brazil.* In "Architectural Review," Feb., 1952.

The Twelve Prophets at Congonhas do Campo. In "The Month," Sept., 1949.

Costa, Lúcio: *Artigos e Estudos de . . . .* Centro de Estudos de Arquitetura. Faculdade de Arquitetura. Universidade do Rio Grande do Sul. Pôrto Alegre, 1954.

Estudos. In "Revista Ante-Projeto," Rio de Janeiro, Apr., 1952.

Sobre Arquitetura. Ier volume, Centros dos Estudantes universitários de Arquitetura da Universidade do Rio Grande do Sul, Pôrto Alegre, 1962.

Engracia, P. Julio: *Relação Chronológica do* Santuário e Irmandade do Senhor Bom Jesus de Congonhas do Campo. São Paulo, 1908.

Falcão, Edgar de Cerqueira: *Reliquias da Bahia.* Brasil. F. Lanzara, São Paulo, 1940.

Reliquias da terra do Ouro. F. Lanzara, São Paulo, 1946.

Goodwin, Philip L.: *Brazil Builds. Architecture Old and New, 1942-1952.* The Museum of Modern Art, New York, 1955.

Hitchcock, Henri-Russel: *Latin American Architecture since 1945.* The Museum of Modern Art, New York, 1955.

Leite, P. Serafim: Artes e ofícios dos Jesuitas no Brasil; 1549-1760. Broteria-Livros de Portugal, Lisboa/Rio de Janeiro, 1953.

Machado, Lourival Gomes and Ayrosa, Eduardo: *Reconquista de Congonhas.* Instituto Nacional do Livro, Rio de Janeiro, 1960.

Machado, Lourival Gomes: *Retrato da Arte Moderna do Brasil.* Gráfica da Prefeitura, São Paulo, 1948.

Mann, Hans: *The 12 Prophets of Antonio Francisco Lisboa, "O Aleijadinho."* Ministério de Educação e Cultura, Serviço de Documentação, Rio de Janeiro, 1958.

Martins, Judith: *Apontamentos para a Bibliographia de Antônio Francisco Lisboa,* in SPHAN, No. 4, 1939.

Mindlin, Henrique: *Modern Architecture in Brazil.* Colibrís ed., Amsterdam/Rio de Janeiro, 1956.

Paglia, Dante: *Arquitetura na Bienal de São Paulo.* Edições Americanas de Arte e Arquitetura, São Paulo, 1951.

Papadaki, Stamo: *The Work of Oscar Niemeyer.* Reinhold, New York, 1950.

Oscar Niemeyer, Works In Progress. Reinhold, New York, 1956.

Oscar Niemeyer, Braziller, New York, 1960.

Reis, José de Sousa: *O Adro do Santuário de Congonhas.* In SPHAN, No. 3, 1939.

Santos, Paulo F.: *A Arquitetura religiosa em* Ouro Preto. Livr. Kosmos, Rio de Janeiro, 1951.

O Barroco e o Jesuítico na Arquitetura do Brasil. Livr. Kosmos, Rio de Janeiro, 1951.

Silva-Nigra, Dom Clemente Maria da: *Artistas coloniais mineiros.* "Revista de História," São Paulo, Yr. 2, No. 6, Apr.-June, 1951.

Smith, Robert C.: *Arquitetura Colonial. As Artes na Bahia.* I. Parte. Livr. Progresso Ed., Bahia, 1955. (Cf. list of 37 works on Brazilian Art in the Valladares introduction to the last book mentioned.)

Acronyms

AIAAIE—*Anales del Instituto de Arte Americano e Investigaciones Estéticas.* Universidad de Buenos Aires. Facultad de Arquitetura y Urbanismo.

AIIE—*Anales del Instituto de Investigaciones Estéticas.* Universidad Autónoma de México.

HLAS—*Handbook of Latin American Studies.* Ed. by the Hispanic Foundation, The Library of Congress and the University of Florida.

RMCh—*Revista Musical Chilena.* Universidad de Chile. Facultad de Ciencias y Artes Musicales.

SPHAN—Serviço do Patrimônio Histórico e Artístico Nacional. Ministério de Educação e Cultura. Rio de Janeiro.

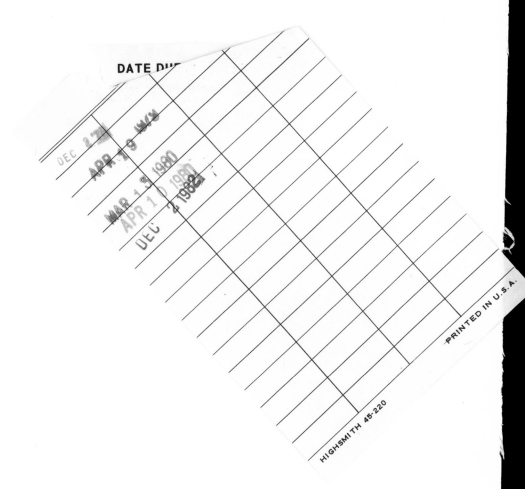

DATE DUE

DEC 2 '79
APR 9 1979
MAR 1 3 1980
APR 1 0 1980
DEC 2 1982

HIGHSMITH 45-220

PRINTED IN U.S.A.

Book design by

TREMONT ASSOCIATES, INC.